THE GOOD Dating Guide

Copyright © Hillie Marshall 1998

All rights reserved.

No part of this book may be reproduced by any means, nor transmitted, nor translated into a machine language without the written permission of the publisher.

Summersdale Publishers
46 West Street
Chichester
West Sussex
PO19 1RP
United Kingdom

A CIP catalogue record for this book is available from the British Library.

ISBN 1 84024 017 2

Printed and bound in Great Britain

TO ANGUS
My ultimate Date

To My Children Nicola and Jamie
Tomorrow's Hot Dates

*With all my thanks to
Stewart, Alastair and Emma
Available on 01243 771107 !*

Contents

Chapter 1 Preparing Yourself For Dating (Sorting Your Mind Out) 13

Chapter 2 Preparing Yourself For Dating (Sorting Your Body Out) 29

Chapter 3 Getting A Date (The Great Challenge) 39

Chapter 4 The First Date (Making The Most Of It) 69

Chapter 5 Dates From Hell! (You Are Not Alone) 91

Chapter 6 The Second Date (The Follow Up, Preparations And Performance) 101

Chapter 7 Taking The Relationship Further (How Far Can You Go, And Keep It Going) 121

Chapter 8 Dating From Scratch In Later Life (It Needn't Be An Itchy Problem!) 141

Conclusion 157

FOREWORD

By Maggie Goodman
(Editor of Home and Life Magazine)

FOREWORD
By Maggie Goodman
(Editor of Home and Life Magazine)

At a time when one in three people live on their own and it gets harder and harder to make casual contacts, Hillie Marshall's new book provides a great service. Some of the most attractive, intelligent and eligible people around find it increasingly difficult to meet other unattached people, because of pressures of work, geography, or simply shyness and lack of self-confidence.

In the late nineties we simply have to put out of our minds any idea that there's something "wrong" with a person who finds it hard to get a date. You can't assume that you will meet your fate in the natural course of things. . . your best bet is to shove chance along a little. In other words, there's never any harm in being in the right place at the right time.

Hillie Marshall is an expert in the subject of finding eligible men, getting a date, and making a great impression on your date, progressing every opportunity and cutting your losses if things don't work out. This book is full of wise and practical advice and every unattached woman who is tired of being on her own should feel inspired and encouraged by it.

The chat-up lines and case histories of "things that can go wrong" and "dates from hell" make this a most entertaining read and will reassure everyone who thinks they're the only one with a problem.

If there's any justice in the world, Hillie's new book should be responsible for lots of happy dates and maybe more than a few happy marriages.

CHAPTER 1

PREPARING YOURSELF FOR DATING

(SORTING YOUR MIND OUT)

There is one golden rule which I have found to be invaluable throughout my life, and that is - ***Every journey is 90% completed in the preparation.*** The journey on the road to successful dating is no exception, and great care should be taken in preparing every aspect of yourself before you attempt to set foot on this adventurous path.

Preparing your Mind

Your whole attitude to yourself, to others, and to life in general, is vitally important. Most people seek those who seem at ease with themselves and doesn't need reassurance because they lack self esteem.

Learn to love yourself!

For some of us this is a pretty tall order and a distinct problem in life!

Here are five ways to learn to love yourself

- Change your way of thinking

- Understand that the world is your mirror

- Be proud of your successes and learn from your mistakes

- Appreciate your good points

- Be less self-critical and don't impose too high a standard on yourself

---

Change your way of thinking

How can you expect someone to love and like you, if *you* don't even love or like yourself? A friend of mine, who was always very outgoing, not only lost her job last year but her self respect along with it. She put on a brave face to start with, but then became very morose and moody, and whenever anyone tried to talk to her she just put herself down. It was very sad to see the change and most of her friends found it difficult to spend time with her. About this time she and I met up for a chat, and I believe I told her what most of her other friends felt they could not. She made a commitment to me that she would do something about her life and change her way of thinking.

Well, she did! She wrote down all her personal attributes and achievements and began to think positively about herself. She constructively researched new avenues of employment and found that other people started looking at her in a new light. Within a few weeks she landed herself another job which was considerably better than the last, and even more importantly she regained her self respect and confidence and once more became the happy person we all remembered.

Understand that the world is your mirror

There is a definite link between how much love you have for yourself and giving love to others. I'm sure you must have noticed many times that when you are smiling and feeling great the whole world seems to smile with you, and life takes on a completely different hue. The fact is that the rest of the world is like a mirror and reflects the way we think about ourselves. When you don't like yourself, you will tend to find fault in others, and they in turn may begin to dislike you. When you like yourself, you will tend to treat others in a fair, understanding and pleasant way which they will appreciate.

Be proud of your successes and learn from your mistakes

Love yourself and others will love you; respect yourself and others will respect you. If you have a healthy self-love you will treat others as you expect to be treated yourself. You will be proud of your successes without feeling that you have constantly to tell everyone else about them, and you will accept and be kind to yourself about your failures, whilst trying to improve yourself. However, if you ever behave in a way that you feel ashamed of, *don't* start loathing yourself. Learn from your mistakes and resolve not to repeat them - don't let them destroy your self worth. Remember that you deserve to be loved and liked and treated well, not because you are a champion tennis player, pop star, or the chairman of a large public company, but because you are *you;* be proud of yourself.

Appreciate your good points

Try making a list of your best qualities, and of all the successes you have achieved throughout your life from as early an age as you can remember. If you take time over this you will be surprised how much you have to be proud about yourself. Subconsciously we all decide how much we are worth, and therefore how much happiness we deserve.

We find we have relationships with people who treat us the way we think we deserve to be treated. If you have a good opinion of yourself, you will expect to be treated well and will not settle for less. If you have a poor opinion of yourself, when life is going really well for you a little voice in the corner of your brain may say 'Hey, hang on a minute, things are too good, something is bound to go wrong!' - and somehow or other things may go wrong because you don't think you deserve very much. If everything goes pear-shaped you will have been proved right, and will probably say to yourself 'I knew it couldn't possibly last!' Don't do this, count your blessings and be optimistic.

Be less self critical and don't impose too high a standard on yourself

Sometimes we become too critical of other people and forget that no one is perfect. It is easy to surmise that everyone else thinks the same way as us, making us more critical of ourselves and setting too high a personal standard to achieve easily. When we don't live up to our own expectations we feel a failure. Fear of failure is a very powerful emotion and extremely destructive. If you can make yourself believe that nothing has to be done or achieved in a specific way then failure becomes impossible. Try watching the actions of a pet animal. A cat will spend all day waiting for and stalking birds, mice, or flies but how often does it get its prey? When it fails, it doesn't lie down and torture itself with feelings of guilt, it immediately gets on with the job of trying to catch the next one. Why not try to learn a few lessons from nature?

Positive Thinking

> ***If you are someone who***
>
> - Constantly looks for things to go wrong
>
> - Feels uncomfortable when things are going well
>
> - Often says 'I would have *if only*....'
>
> - Tends to blame others or circumstances for your misfortunes
>
> - Nit-picks at others' shortcomings instead of appreciating their good points
>
> ***You are tending towards negativity.***

The first step towards positivity is to recognise that things can't go your way 100% of the time - but neither can they go against you 100% of the time. Be prepared for this and don't become paralysed by negativity.

> ***Six ways positively to change your life***
>
> - Change your attitude
>
> - *Thought-block* negative thoughts

- Be positive when you speak
- Consider each problem as a challenge
- Use your mind as a *positive* magnet
- Change your negative patterns

Change your attitude

It is never too late to change. Take your first big step forward in life and change your attitude. You can't change others but you *can* change yourself. Change the way you think and talk about yourself and surround yourself with *good* and *positive* people. Think yourself a winner and you will be. If you constantly tell yourself you can't do something or you are hopeless, then you are giving yourself no chance whatsoever. Change your vocabulary to *I can; I will; I shall be successful;* and you can move mountains, for anything is possible.

Thought-block negative thoughts

From this very second you can start to eliminate doubts from your mind and your conversation. Every time a negative fear enters your mind, *thought-block* it out. By this I mean immediately concentrate your thoughts onto other happier prospects and plans, and mentally forbid those negative doubts.

Be positive when you speak

Banish the word *can't* from your vocabulary: start saying *I can*. Don't talk about what you don't want or don't have, start talking about what you want. Stop thinking and talking about what could go wrong in a situation, and start planning how you are going to make everything come right. Never think of failure, because by so doing you can attract it. If you have a set-back, welcome it as a useful learning exercise towards future success. Mistakes are just errors of judgement which *anyone* could have made. Remember it is better to have done *something* and failed, than never even having tried.

Consider each problem as a challenge

Start thinking of problems as a challenge and an opportunity to learn. If the great inventors of our time hadn't made countless mistakes, learnt from them, made more mistakes but still progressed forward, we probably wouldn't have advanced past the caveman era. Be enthusiastic about life, and don't ever stop striving to improve yourself until the day you die - even then you can probably start a new and exciting challenge in a different dimension.

Use your mind as a positive magnet

We have the power to attract the good or the bad in any situation. Our minds act like magnets. If you concentrate your thoughts on what you want to happen, and constantly re-create that happy scenario in your mind, it probably will. If you fear something you will automatically attract it.

Even saying the words 'I don't want this to happen' can make your mind go towards it. How often have you said to yourself 'I mustn't dirty this clean shirt because I haven't got another to wear for my job interview' or 'I must be careful not to ladder my tights because this is my last pair' and you pretty soon spill your cup of coffee down your shirt, or accidentally rip your tights.

The same thing happens in our relationships when we are afraid of losing our partner. The very fact that we even think about losing their love and affection puts us on a dangerous course. We must just concentrate on and enjoy what we have now, and leave the future to take care of itself.

Change your negative patterns

You may be someone who is always broke, always late, always in a mess, always having accidents, always has the flu three times a year or gets a headache every Sunday night; always has a drama happening in your life. You *can* change your way of life: you can become someone who says 'I'm always healthy'; 'life is good to me'; 'life is fun'. Be positive and make plans to achieve new goals to change your finances. Stop doing everything at the last moment and reorganise yourself to have enough time to be *on time*. Eliminate the danger of having accidents because you are always in a rush. Banish the very idea of getting ill from your mind - it is a well known fact that many people have overcome serious illness with just sheer will-power and positive thinking. Start organising your life so that you are not stressed into living in a constant state of disorder.

Learn to be Happy

It is such a pleasure to be with someone who is genuinely happy in themselves, someone who hasn't got the weight of the world on their shoulders and who appreciates being with *you*.

Seven ways to learn to be happy

- Change the way you react to circumstances
- Recognise and change your destructive behaviour
- Think happy
- Eliminate approval seeking and jealous feelings
- Accept and make the most of what you have
- Make time for yourself
- Enjoy now

Change the way you react to circumstances

Being happy has a lot to do with the way we react to circumstances. One man's disaster could be another man's road to success. For example, someone, on hearing that they were jobless, might collapse into despair. Someone else given the same circumstances, might decide that fate was giving them the greatest opportunity of their life. They might investigate the possibilities of a new career and begin training for an even better job than before; they might even move to a completely new area to give themselves a fresh start. React positively with an open mind to a challenge and give yourself the chance of success.

Every cloud has a silver lining!

Recognise and change your destructive behaviour

Being happy can be the most difficult achievement in life. Many of us feel uncomfortable and off-balance when life is going well for us. Many a relationship is unwittingly sabotaged by one partner, because they only feel at ease with failure and with being a victim. If you recognise yourself here, make time to think about your problem and how you can change yourself. You may decide to seek help in order to find out why you behave the way you do, but in the end it is up to *you*.

If you really want to be happy, then tell yourself right now that you *are* going to be happy and that you will not let any destructive element in you get in the way. Make a concentrated effort to recognise your destructive behaviour and really determine to stop it. In fact you need a lot of determination to be happy, and to challenge and get rid of every unhappy thought that enters your mind.

Think happy

It is within your capability to be happy. You *can* do what you want to do, go where you want to go, see who and what you want to see, so empower yourself by making these choices for yourself. The road to happiness can start as simply as spending time with happy, sociable people and thought-blocking any thoughts of sadness and negativity.

Eliminate approval seeking and jealous feelings

Happy people do not need to seek the approval of others to give them a sense of value, because they have self esteem and are secure in themselves. Jealousy is an insecurity in ourselves, a feeling that we are worth a lesser amount of love than others. It is a put-down of ourselves; it is a lack of trust in ourselves and the other person, and can never bring happiness. Love yourself enough not to let someone else's behaviour cause you emotional discomfort.

Accept and make the most of what you have

A happy person makes the most of what they have got, and will be happy with their lot. Try to recognise that the world and the people in it are not perfect, and that you can't change that fact. If you can accept the way things *are*, instead of the way you think things *should* be, and enjoy every precious present moment you have you will find a tremendous weight is lifted off your shoulders. People will be attracted to your light, and you'll find being happy inside is possibly the best chat-up technique you could ever acquire!

Make time for yourself (Get a life!)

These days people are having to work longer and more unsociable hours because of the economic climate, and life becomes all work and no play. They have no idea how much they are missing out on life until it is too late. A successful career does not ensure stability and happiness. Don't sacrifice your personal life for your career, instead take time to explore all that life has to offer.

Down-shifting.
This is currently receiving a lot attention. It is a method by which people decide what they actually *need* to be comfortable and happy, and don't strive for more. Instead of struggling to move a few rungs up the ladder in order to get a bigger house, a bigger car, and a bigger mortgage they endeavour to move themselves several rungs down the ladder. They are opting out of the rat-race in order to gain more time and personal freedom for themselves, sacrificing material luxuries for a far more pleasant and fulfilling life-style. I think this makes a lot of sense. If *you* are overworked, fraught with anxiety, stressed beyond all sensible bounds with no opportunity to make a social life for yourself, why don't you get a piece of paper and write down what is important and necessary for you to exist comfortably. What could *you* give up in order to achieve a less stressful and more fulfilling life?

Enjoy* now *(There's no time to waste)
As I have mentioned before, the present moment is the only *real* moment we will ever experience. So why waste it? Amidst regrets about the past and worries about the future the present moment goes by unnoticed most of the time. Worrying about something in the future is not going to make it better, and torturing yourself with regrets will not *right a wrong*. You have to move forward and learn a lesson

from past mistakes. Everyone makes mistakes, but clever people learn from them and make sure that they never happen again.

Don't constantly plan for the future; plotting the day when somehow you will have the time to do everything you have ever wanted to do, when life will be so much better and happier than it is now. Life just passes by when you are wrapped up in the mythical future. Instead realise that *now* is all any of us will ever have.

Gaining Self Confidence

Probably deep down most of us are unsure of ourselves, and lack self confidence.

Six ways to help gain self confidence

- Improve your feelings of self-worth

- Realise that you are not unique - others are nervous as well

- Don't be fearful of what others may think of you

- Never put yourself down

- Learn to receive compliments

- Fake confidence

Improve your feelings of self-worth
As suggested earlier in this chapter, make a list of all your attributes and achievements, try to believe in yourself and give yourself some mental praise. Always remember that *you* determine your own worth, and that your worth has absolutely nothing to do with your actions or the way you feel about things. Sometimes you won't like the way you behaved but this has nothing to do with your worth. Learn from your mistakes and determine to do better next time, but don't lose confidence in your self-worth.

Realise that you are not unique - others are nervous as well
Whatever image someone may care to portray, I don't think that anyone is entirely self confident. We all get nervous in varying situations, and if you can concentrate on putting others at their ease instead of concentrating on your own unease, they will respond well to you and you will begin to feel more confident.

Don't be fearful of what others may think of you
Have the courage of your convictions to do what you feel is right for you, providing you don't hurt anyone else in doing so. It doesn't matter what others think of you - we can't be everyone's favourite person. Face the fact that not everyone in this life is going to like you or your actions, so you might as well go with your own gut feelings and get on with what you want to do.

Never put yourself down
Putting yourself down through your conversation or actions does nothing to enhance your image. Don't boast or brag,

but always say good and positive things about yourself. If you concentrate on the best in you, not only will this give you more self confidence, but it will instil a sense of well-being in whoever you are with at the time. It is depressing to be with someone who portrays themselves as a loser, and who could also appear to be *fishing for compliments*. Of course, if you resolve to be *happy* and think happy and positive thoughts, you will portray a happy, 'together' personality.

Learn to receive compliments
Try to develop the habit of accepting compliments with good grace and a thank you. People who give you their compliments feel good about giving them to you; don't disappoint them by throwing their gift back in their face by telling them that they were wrong in their assessment of you. Accept what they say and give your self esteem a boost.

Fake confidence
Another way I have found to help *my* self confidence is to fake it. Many people as they become more successful or famous begin to feel less confident in themselves as they wonder how they can keep up with their public image. However, because they have become so adept at faking confidence, the likes of you and I would probably never guess at their own insecurities. I'm sure that after a few months of acting out a self confident *you*, you would probably find that you have even convinced *yourself!*

CHAPTER 2

PREPARING YOURSELF FOR DATING

(SORTING YOUR BODY OUT)

Having prepared your mind, you need to prepare your body.

> ***Four ways to prepare your body***
>
> - Think yourself attractive
> - Be healthy
> - Learn to like your body
> - Identify what you don't like and change it

Think yourself attractive

To be successful in dating you need the confidence to know you are looking your best and most attractive. Please don't imagine here that I am advocating that you should all aspire to superstar looks in order to be successful. People are attracted to the whole person, and most of that attractiveness or beauty will shine out from within. Have confidence in your personality, and just think of yourself as one of the sexiest and most attractive people around, and you *will* be. Positive thinking really works!

Be healthy

It is no good looking great and being a 'together' person, if you are always unavailable to date because of ill health. So do your best to prevent illness entering your life. Get enough sleep, enough healthy exercise, eat healthy food, surround yourself with enthusiastic, positive, healthy people, and always think yourself well.

You owe it to yourself to be healthy!

Learn to like your body
Anyone looking at themselves naked in the mirror will find some part of their body to criticise. The fact is that none of us is perfect, but it is worth remembering that everyone has different tastes. One woman might be turned on by short, fat, balding men, whilst another might fancy skinny, hairy giants! Just because fashion magazines suggest that certain images are the ones we should all strive to achieve, this does not necessarily mean that they are right. Bear in mind that most of us look our most attractive with our own natural body weight: Marilyn Monroe certainly did! Try to learn to *accept* your differences rather than condemn them. Someone somewhere will think they are perfect for them.

I am sure you must, at some stage in your life, have seen someone you considered to be exceedingly unattractive, arm in arm and looking blissfully happy with the most stunning creature you have ever witnessed. 'What on earth does she see in him?' you think to yourself. Maybe the stunning creature has brains as well as beauty, recognising a beautiful person beneath those unattractive looks, so that that person becomes exceedingly attractive to them?

Identify what you don't like

Is it your
- Weight
- Posture
- Face
- Hair
- Image

Weight

Ways to control weight
- Exercise
- Diet

Exercise

Exercise will not only tone up your body contours, but it will give you more energy, more zest for life, and also help subdue hunger pangs. Join a local health club and work out in the gym, swim, or play a sport such as tennis or squash, at least three times a week.

However, if this is too expensive, you will find most areas have public sports facilities you can visit whenever you like for a very modest cost. You could also try using an exercise video, or jogging around the streets or country lanes which would cost you nothing at all.

Diet

Always check with your doctor before you decide to go on a diet. He will be able to advise you about healthy ways to diet and may even refer you to a dietician. Whenever I have wanted to lose weight, I have always found it beneficial to forget the word *diet* because it just focuses your mind on food. Use common sense to change slowly the way you eat for the long term.

Strictly depriving yourself of all your favourite foods and sticking to a rigid diet will usually only last for a few days before you go back to your old habits. However, if you do have a 'binge', be understanding and kind to yourself. Don't mentally whip yourself and get depressed. Remember that eating healthily, unlike strict dieting, is flexible, always positive and will help avoid 'comfort eating'. A useful tip I was once told is to go and brush your teeth with toothpaste every time you feel the urge to eat a box of chocolates or a similar treat - I tried it and it really does work.

Check that you aren't eating as a displacement activity. Often it's easier to head for the fridge than do something you're not looking forward to. Write a list each day of the things that you need to do and cross each item off as you do it. Seeing the list diminish will spur you on and give you enormous encouragement. You'll find you don't have time to over-eat. Many people over-eat because they are just plain bored. The remedy for this is to shake off the lethargy and do something - play sports, join a class, meet friends, go to the theatre, museums, *anything!* Try to eat three healthy balanced meals a day with no eating in between.

If you feel that you are too thin, go and see your GP to make sure the problem isn't a medical one. Also, think about your lifestyle - stress is a major contributor to weight loss.

If you are feeling very flush, then why not really pamper yourself and go to a health farm for a few days. You will not only lick your body into shape but you will come away looking and feeling great.

Whatever you decide to do about your weight, don't become a diet bore! Remember that whether you are size 8 or size 18, if you feel comfortable and attractive with your figure, there is absolutely no reason why you should seek to change it.

Posture

Good posture is essential for making your body look good. If you hunch your shoulders and slouch, or stick your tummy out, you are not portraying yourself at your best. Exercise will help your posture, as will massages to help rid you of tense tight muscles. The Alexander technique is also an excellent way to help correct bad posture. Ask your local health club or fitness centre for details of local instructors.

Face

> ### *Seven ways to improve your facial looks*
>
> - Eat a healthy diet
> - Get enough sleep
> - Control your alcohol intake
> - Stop smoking
> - Protect your face from the sun
> - Have regular dental check-ups
> - Consult a beautician

Eat a healthy diet

Eat plenty of healthy foods such as fresh fruit and vegetables, and avoid sugary and starchy products which could give you spots and a pasty complexion. Eating a healthy diet and drinking plenty of water can help ensure that you have bright eyes, a spot free face and a healthy coloured complexion.

Get enough sleep

It is essential to get enough sleep to avoid having dull, tired-looking eyes with dark circles underneath. Repeated lack of sleep is also very ageing to your looks. On the subject of eyes, do have regular eye tests, and if you need to purchase a pair of glasses take a friend along with you to help choose the most attractive pair for you.

Control your alcohol intake

Keeping your alcohol intake to the minimum will help avoid a red nose, blotchy dry skin and bleary eyes!

Stop smoking

Smoking produces ageing lines on your face, a dry skin, and bad breath. Remember, not many people like kissing an ash-tray.

Protect your face from the sun

Although having a tan will make you feel good (whether it's gained naturally from the sun or artificially from a sun-bed), you could land up with a lined, aged face. Try to keep your tanning to a minimum, and always wear a protective sun-screen cream in the sun. Wear sunglasses in sunny weather to protect your eyes, and remember they're also useful for discreet ogling on the beach.

Have regular dental check-ups

Do visit your dentist and dental hygienist regularly to make sure you haven't got any dental problems to give your breath an odour which not even your best friend could tell you about. Also remember you will be a lot more kissable if you have an attractive and sparkling clean set of teeth.

Consult a beautician

Take some professional advice from a beautician as to which moisturisers would be best for your skin, and which make-up will suit you best. Don't wear heavy make-up - most men prefer a natural look, not a painted doll. When you have found a look that makes you feel really good and attractive, stick to it - whatever else fashion may dictate. Also give yourself the occasional treat and have a facial massage - great for the looks and morale whichever sex you are.

Hair

You will probably appeal to more people if you have clean, conditioned, well cut hair, although there is no reason why you shouldn't experiment! Of course it's Sod's law that the one day you decide to go out with lank greasy hair will be when you meet the woman/man of your dreams. Follow hair fashions if you wish (and it is good once in a while to change your image) but do make sure that whatever hairstyle you decide to have is right for *you*. If you want to change your hair colour, I would advise you to get advice from your hairdresser as to the right colour for you, and get it professionally done to avoid hair nightmares! It is always worth going to the best hairdresser you can afford to get the best treatment for your hair.

In my opinion, men who have thinning hair should not try to disguise it. If you are bald avoid wearing a hairpiece - it's usually noticeable, and will probably come off at the worst possible moment. Just accept the fact that most men lose their hair, it is a natural life process so make the best of it. I think that most women would appreciate a natural rather than artificial look. Possibly the most effective way to minimise your baldness is to have a very short haircut, so that the thinning parts do not stand out so much.

Facial hair is a turn off for some, and a definite turn on for others. Remember that stubble could give your kissing partner a painful red blotchy rash on her face, and I imagine she would not thank you for it! Make sure that your moustache or beard is neatly trimmed, and remember that a beard covered in beer foam is usually very off-putting!

Image

If you really want to look your best, it is worthwhile investing some money in an image consultant who will advise you which are the best and most attractive colours for your skin colouring, and which are the colours you should avoid. They will also advise you on the best styles of clothing for your body shape. It is always better to have a few well cut clothes that really suit you and make you feel good, than a wardrobe full of cheap fashionable clothes that don't really do much to enhance your image.

Finally, remember the one thing you wear which will have the biggest impact on other people is your expression. Someone who has a happy cheerful look will fare much better than someone who looks miserable, fed-up and bored with themselves. Notice how you tend to approach people who make you laugh and have a sunny disposition, with a light heart and jovial manner. If this is the effect other people have on you, then learn to develop your own personality and expressions so that people are pleased to see you and immediately smile with pleasure.

CHAPTER 3

GETTING A DATE
(*THE GREAT CHALLENGE*)

Having prepared yourself physically and mentally, you're now ready for the big step of finding a Date. Half the challenge of finding your dream Date is knowing where to look, so it's worth planning ahead.

Where to Find your Date

Where do you find your ideal partner? The short answer is - anywhere! Chances are that you will meet someone you really want to date when you least expect it, so you should always be on your toes and try to look your best wherever you are. But don't sit around waiting for fate to walk round the corner! You can help speed things up a bit by strategically placing yourself in some likely locations. Finding someone to date is a numbers game. The more you put yourself about, and the more people you meet, the more chance you have of success. Choose an environment where you're most likely to meet your type of person, and the chances are it will also be a place where you'll be at your most friendly and relaxed. For example you are unlikely to meet a hardcore raver at an evening class for flower arranging or a studious, home-loving academic at the latest, trendy nightclub.

Eight avenues to investigate.
If you're not sure of the effectiveness of this ploy, think of all the romantic situations in which couples have first met in films - *Sleepless in Seattle*, *Shirley Valentine* and *Brief Encounter* to name but a few!

Eight places to find a date

- Friends
- Sport
- Clubs, pubs and wine bars
- Work
- Classes and societies
- Holidays
- Agencies
- Adverts

Friends

Parties, dinner parties, drinks parties or any kind of get-together organised by friends, are ideal events to meet a potential Date. Your friends hopefully know *you* very well, and may have already selected a short list of possibilities for your delectation. The advantage of events organised by friends is that the ice is invariably broken for you - you already have something in common and can be easily introduced to whomever you wish without having to decide how to the make the approach. Use this advantage in order to make an immediate impression. You're already 'intimate' so spend the rest of the evening becoming more so!

Better still, as you know everyone's relationship status, you're not going to waste any passionate glances in the direction of someone who's attached.

However, be careful, as a relationship within a circle of friends can quickly become the topic of widespread gossip and speculation, and although they probably have your best interests at heart, too much interference can sometimes add quite a lot of pressure at the start of a new relationship. Furthermore, if your date goes horribly wrong, he or she will be around to serve as a frequent reminder of the failure and your friends might also be put in an awkward position about split loyalties.

Sports

A health club or sports club serves two purposes: it is an extremely good place to meet other single people, and you will get trim, fit and healthy in the process. Who else but a single person would usually have so much time or money to devote to thrashing their bodies in the gym, swimming pool, squash court etc? It's a well known fact that you can pull more than a muscle working out! You will also get to see a bit more of them in their lycras or swimming trunks and such 'inside knowledge' can often be worth its weight in gold when meeting someone for the first time.

If you are keen on sport already, you will meet others with whom you have a lot in common. You will also have plenty of time to get to know them over 18 holes of golf, a tennis tournament or pumping iron in the gym. Sports clubs and health clubs are also usually heavily into arranging social activities, such as parties, walks, tournaments, games or holidays. You might even find it profitable to spend your time at the club attractively propping up the bar, chatting up or being chatted up!

Cunning tacticians could take up a sport traditionally dominated by the opposite sex. A man will surely be surrounded by lycra-clad women if he takes up aerobics! Many of the traditional male sports such as football and golf are now being taking up by women, but how about some fly-fishing or joining in a clay pigeon shoot?

Clubs, Pubs and Bars

Nightclubs have certain advantages - the lack of lighting makes everyone (including yourself) appear more attractive than usual. This effect can be heightened further with a few glasses of alcohol. The loud music also takes away the need for that tortuous first conversation - instead let your feet do the talking and if you like the look of someone on the dance floor, a few strategic disco moves can neatly place you in their vicinity.

Women can get dressed up and look glamorous and if you don't dance too energetically, your make-up shouldn't run. Do, however, be aware that these advantages can misfire. You could be swept off your feet by a dazzling, mysterious hunk one evening, yet on the next meeting, discover the reality to be a lot less appealing. Remember that however irresistible they may seem, anyone with a wedding ring on their finger will only bring pain in the future.

> **Also be sensible and don't accept a lift from a complete stranger or take them home with you.**

Pubs and wine bars are usually better lit but probably just as hectic. It is quite daunting to go into a busy bar on your own as most people will be there with a group of friends. So why not get a group of your friends together and choose somewhere popular on a Friday night, or at the weekend. If the place is really crowded then you will be able to get quite close to someone who you like the look of and you will be able to see how they socialise with their friends. You may well find yourself crammed in at the bar next to a possible Date.

Work

You will have your job and day to day happenings as a common interest with anyone you meet at work. You would have been able to observe them at close quarters and to find out a lot about them from their colleagues. Hopefully you'll both finish work at the same time and it will be easy to meet up for a date. If an office romance is what you really want and you know who you want it to be with, the notorious office party (where fellow work mates suddenly let their hair down and become wild creatures) is probably the place to begin! However, be careful of doing anything you might regret.

Sometimes it's best not to mix business with pleasure. If you go out with someone from work and the relationship breaks up badly, you will find it extremely difficult and awkward to be confronted with each other every day at work. It's an unfortunate sign of the times that office relationships can tread uncomfortably close to the line of 'sexual harassment'.

Classes and Societies

Learning a new skill, subject or language at an evening class can be another way of meeting like-minded people. Societies, such as amateur dramatic societies, can be a great source of fun and a good place to meet single people. You are united in the common cause of putting on the production, and will be spending a lot of time together especially in the final stages.

Of course, if you land up playing the romantic lead opposite a particularly dashing thespian take every opportunity of rehearsing your love scenes, and hopefully staged passion will become increasingly easy to recreate. However, you are probably more likely to form a lasting liaison in the less romantic regions backstage. It's always worth bearing in mind that these romances often last only the length of the project you are working on, and frequently, with classes, the number of potential dates may dwindle as many of the students decide there is nobody attending the class that they fancy!

If you are interested in stamp collecting, bee keeping, or anything else, I suggest you enquire at your local library or look in the local paper. Men might do well to join a sewing class, and women might do well to join a car mechanics class. . .

Dance classes are particularly popular at the moment. Salsa, ballroom and line dancing classes are a great way to meet other singles in a fun and informal environment. What's more, they are surprisingly cheap and so popular that some are bound to be held in your area. You can learn the moves and make them if you want to!

Chance Meetings in Other Locations

It is surprising how many people meet each other in the most unlikely places, such as over the frozen peas section at the local supermarket. In fact if you think about it, a supermarket is a very good place to hang out to meet other single people as they all have to eat and probably cook for themselves. Take a quick peek in a likely candidate's basket - microwave meals for one and a four pack of lager may well mean they are single.

Libraries could be another place to hunt out dates if you're interested in mental stimulation, but watch out for the hawk-eyed librarians.

Public transport, such as buses and trains, is also somewhere to keep your eyes open for the Date. The boredom factor comes into play on long bus or train journeys, and you may find it's not too difficult to get someone to talk to you. The underground service is ideal because it is usually jammed full of every conceivable type of person and you are certainly close enough to them.

Planes are a great environment to get to know someone you're sitting next to, especially if it's a long haul flight. Also always keep your eyes open in the street, walking in the park, indeed anywhere you know there will be other human beings!

The only negative aspect to this ad-lib method of getting a Date is that you are approaching a stranger in an unfamiliar environment. They may be very suspicious or even resent your amorous intrusion, or worse still they may turn out to be a nutter. Be careful - appearances can be deceptive.

Holidays

People on holiday are much more at ease, carefree, and open to suggestions than they might be in a normal social circumstance. If there is a language barrier there won't be too much talking going on and you may reach a point of physical communication quicker. There are singles package holidays you could go on, or resorts that mainly cater for single people both at home and abroad. Look in the newspaper and ask at your local travel agent.

It's important to remember that the euphoria of a holiday romance is, more often than not, short lived - but don't let that stop you from enjoying the time you have with your holiday partner to the full.

I know of three builders from Bolton who bought a farmhouse in the South of France and converted it to a restaurant. One of the first customers to this restaurant was a Dutch tourist and she subsequently fell in love with one of the builders. He left the restaurant, she left Holland and they now live together in Northern France where he's started a building firm. Neutral territory!

Agencies

Dating agencies are another way to find a Date. The reputable ones will have screened their clients to make sure they are everything they purport to be and that they are single. They will also hopefully introduce you to Dates who are of an age you wish to meet and with similar interests.

I understand that with some agencies you look through photos and profiles of their clients, make your choice and hope that they will reciprocate, and another member might in turn make you their choice. With other agencies you leave it up to them to make the contacts for you. This is all obviously less hassle than having to find someone yourself.

Admittedly, this manner of finding a date could be thought of as cold and unromantic. You must also consider the worst possible scenario - just imagine turning up to meet your Date and being forced to spend an evening with someone you find physically and mentally repugnant. Be sparing with your personal details, just in case he/she decides that you are THE ONE for them and determines to convince you of this with pestering calls or visits.

You must also make sure that the agency is a reputable one; has preferably been trading for at least three years under their *present* name; that it has a proven track record; has enough suitable clients to introduce you to; that they also guarantee to give you at least a set amount of introductions. Be very wary of anyone promising you your future spouse because no one can make that kind of promise, and do *not* be persuaded into parting with large sums of money to an agency. It is *never* the case that the more money you spend on finding a partner, the better that partner will be!

You could also try a Dining and Social Events agency. Here you will meet single people in groups at dinner parties, buffets, social events and activities, and be able to go on weekend breaks and holidays with them.

This has the advantage of:

- Safety in numbers (personal safety, and the boredom factor of being stuck with one unsuitable person).

- Being a more natural way of meeting the opposite sex.

- Becoming a fashionable way to meet new friends.

- Having virtually no stigma attached.

- Being a great way to visit new venues you might not normally think of going to.

- Being able to make friends of the same sex for you to go hunting with (they might also have friends of the opposite sex they could introduce you to whom they don't fancy but you might).

This way of meeting new friends can also be a marvellous stepping stone back into society if you have just broken up with a partner, and it may help you to get back some of your confidence about being single once more.

Again make sure that the agency has been trading under its *present* name for at least three years; that it has a proven track record; that it has plenty of clients of the opposite sex and of the right age; that all its dinners and social events have equal numbers of both sexes attending; that none of your personal details are ever given out to anyone without your permission.

> **Also, please be aware that, to my knowledge, there is no official independent controlling body overseeing the proper running of introduction agencies.**

Adverts

You can advertise for a Date in many newspapers and magazines under the personal column section and use one of their box numbers. You will probably have hundreds of replies and get so many dates you won't have time to do anything else.

The majority of the time you will enjoy meeting lots of new dates, but don't rely on many of them being suitable for you. You may waste many valuable hours, days, weeks and months sifting through people you would never normally dream of dating. There is also no middle contact to vet the Date for you, and the usual dangers of going out with a stranger apply: they may be married; just out for a one-night stand; an undesirable character. Always make sure you meet your Date in a public place, and let a friend know what you are up to.

How to Secure a Date

You see someone you like, what do you do next?

> ### *Five questions you may ask yourself*
>
> - Should you make the first move?
> - What do you do?
> - What do you say?
> - How do you interpret their body language?
> - How do you ask for a date?

Should you make the first move?

The first thing you have to do, if you want to get to know someone you see and like, is to make contact. Chances are they may not have noticed you, and so if you wait for them to make the first move you could be waiting for an awfully long time. You will also save a lot of valuable time by finding out as soon as possible whether there is a mutual attraction or not. If there isn't, you will have lost nothing by making the first move but instead will have gained time to look for someone else who does find you attractive. I had a letter some time ago from a girl who wrote:

> 'I really like a man who works across the road from my office, but I don't know what to do about it. I am rather shy and not at all confident when it comes to relationships. I see him quite often and he smiles at me, and I have been told that he asks his work colleagues about me but says he is too shy to ask me out! I can't ask him out because I am afraid of being rejected. Maybe I should just leave it, but I really like him and want to get to know him better. What do you think?'

I told her to go for it; she had nothing to lose and everything to gain. I gather from her thank you letter to me some months later that they are now very happily going out together.

If things should not go well, try not to feel rejected or put off by a rebuff. Everyone I know has faced rejection. Both sexes have tremendous anxiety about rejection, and so maybe that is why the person you fancy is not approaching you first.

Rejection is a fact of life; it is how you cope with it that is important.

One friend of mine still shudders when he remembers a night at his local nightclub. He saw a girl he thought was gorgeous, plucked up his courage and squeezed past a line of ten of her girlfriends all sitting close together, to ask her for a dance. He asked her and she said 'No!' and turned away. He then had to turn round and squeeze past the ten girlfriends who were by now all looking at him with curiosity and suspicion, and he retreated to the bar. He felt humiliated, rejected and wanted to leave, but I gather he stayed and after a few pints felt better.

What he now realises is that there could have been a number of reasons why this girl turned him down. She might have been expecting a jealous boyfriend to arrive any minute; she could have been married; maybe she felt ill; maybe it was the wrong time of the month; maybe she'd broken the heel of one of her shoes; or maybe she was just unpleasant and bad mannered and therefore he was better off without her!

However much we want someone we find attractive to like us, it isn't always possible because we all have different tastes and cannot be expected to fancy the world in general. If you are rejected try not to view it as a personal insult, just bear in mind that the real reason probably has nothing to do with you at all. Mentally shrug your shoulders and move on.

Traditionally, men are expected to make the first move and women to wait passively to be won over. However, research has shown that in two-thirds of all meetings it is women who, in a subtle way, engineered them. Also in the majority of cases, the men they lured were convinced that *they* had made the first move and were proud of their achievement!

Most importantly, if you want someone to approach you, be approachable and easy to talk to. If you are a fun, relaxed and caring person and you are happy with yourself and your lot in life then people, almost certainly, will be drawn to you like a magnet.

What do you do to make contact?

> **Five ways to make contact**
> - Friends
> - Smiling
> - Eyes
> - Writing
> - Collision

Friends

If you have the advantage of knowing a mutual friend you can get them to introduce you. Most people, especially women, will feel more comfortable and relaxed when they are approached by someone who has been vetted rather than by a complete stranger. If you can therefore establish any link between yourself and the person you wish to know, it is worth its weight in gold.

Smiling

If you are not fortunate enough to be introduced by someone else, sometimes the simplest and easiest way to make contact is just to smile. Few people can resist a genuine friendly smile, especially one full of admiration, and it usually results in a friendly smile back. Your smile has let them know that you are interested and find them attractive, and you will be able to tell by the way they smile back at you whether they are returning the compliment. If their smile is a brief one showing no emotion and they immediately turn their attention elsewhere, you would be better off to turn your attentions elsewhere. However, if their smile is brief but they blush, look coy or embarrassed, or if they return a beaming *I'm so pleased you like me too* smile, you could be on a winning ticket.

Eyes

Eye contact is a powerful way of getting someone's attention, especially *the five second gaze and smile*. The reaction is usually instantaneous and they may well approach you. If it results in a glare you've lost nothing except for five seconds of your time.

Writing

Sometimes, if you feel too shy to make a physical approach, it is easier to put your interest in writing. Many a romance has started via e-mail on the internet. Whatever you decide to write keep it short, light-hearted and amusing. A note that brings a smile to the face will be far more likely to bring results than a heavy, deep or slushy one. If you feel so inclined you could write a love poem. Robert Browning and other famous poets certainly achieved their objectives in this way, and you might even consider copying some of their poetry. However, a stupid ditty like:

> *Roses are red,*
> *And so is your car,*
> *Let's meet for a drink,*
> *And we could go far!*

might serve equally well. Failing that, you could buy *Classic Love Poems* published by my publishers - Summersdale!

Collision

A friend of mine was so desperate to make contact with a man she fancied from afar, that she literally lay in wait for him one evening after work. She waited for him to come out of his office and ran towards him clutching a bag of shopping plus her briefcase as if she were running to catch her bus or train, and accidentally bumped into him. Of course the shopping went flying, bottles were broken, papers were flung out of her briefcase and he was mortified that he had caused such a disaster. He insisted on helping her to clear things up and asked her out for a drink to make amends. This was certainly a somewhat desperate plan on her behalf, but one which worked. In fact bumping into someone, whether it be with your trolley in the supermarket, or falling over their feet on the dance floor, will always produce a result - hopefully (if you manage it the right way) a good one.

What do you say?

Having made contact you need to open up a conversation and there is no point in agonising over what you should say - anything will do, even *hello* will do to get the dialogue going. Imagine that the other person is more nervous than you are, and try to put them at their ease. A word of warning here - if you feel you need an alcoholic drink to give you Dutch courage then have one, but only have just enough to loosen your inhibitions. Few people like to be chatted up by someone who has had one too many. If you feel you need chat-up lines to get you going make sure they are simple, or outrageous enough to make him/her laugh. However, be warned, contrived chat up lines are more likely to make the recipient cringe than open up to your advance.

Getting a Date

Twenty sample chat-up lines

- Let's skip the awkward beginning and pretend we've known each other for a while. So how's your Mum?

- Are your legs tired? You've been running through my mind all day.

- I was watching you for a while and do you know what I like most about you? All of you.

- Hi. I'm on a computer date tonight but the computer hasn't shown up. Would you like to join me instead?

- Could you recommend a good chat-up line? (repeat what he/she says)

- Believe me, I've tried to come up with an original chat-up line, but it's really difficult. Now that I'm already talking to you though, I might as well carry on!

- If I had created the alphabet, I would have put *U* and *I* together.

- I've never chatted anybody up before. Will you teach me?

- Forgive me for being so forward, but may I introduce myself?

- Please talk to me so that girl/man over there will leave me alone.

- You probably think that I'm mad coming up to you like this, but I have this strange urge to buy you a drink.

- If I told you that you have a beautiful body, would you hold it against me?

- Nobody I know can tell me who you are, but I'm sure I've seen you before.

- My friends said that you would definitely turn me down if I asked you for a drink. Help me prove them wrong?

- Can I help you with that? (heavy shopping etc.)

- Could you help me with this please? (heavy shopping etc.)

- Would you accept my last Rollo? (make sure you have one!)

- Umpteen people must have told you this, but you're very beautiful.

- Would you like to hear my best chat up line? (yes) That was it!

- What would you do if you ever got chatted up by a woman?

Getting a Date

However, sometimes it's not *what* you say but the *way* that you say it. For example at one of my *Dinner Dates* dinner parties, a female guest was approached by the waiter who said 'Horseradish, madam?' in such a sexy voice that she was completely hooked. She had eyes for no one except this man all night and I gather they are living blissfully together now.

Eight general conversation guide lines

- Be a good listener.

- Avoid recounting your life history.

- Silence is seldom golden.

- Be amusing without going over the top.

- Being dismissive or a people pleaser will rarely impress.

- Keep a sense of humour.

- Be positive.

- Being too forceful can be a turn off.

Be a good listener

Always show an interest in the person you are talking to and be a good listener. Try to remember that their sister's name is Gertrude and their father has a gammy leg! It is also very unflattering to the other person if you repeat a question later in the conversation that they have already answered; your apparent disinterest in what they have been saying could make them disinterested in you. People like to talk about themselves and are flattered when others are interested by what they say.

Avoid recounting your life history
Try not to be someone who nervously talks non stop about themselves because they feel they have to keep the conversation going at all costs; you may find you have nothing left to talk about at a future date.

It is always better to keep some things about you in reserve.

Silence is seldom golden
Try not to be silent to the extent that it seems you have nothing of interest to say about yourself. Also, if the other person lands up doing all the talking they might get tired and bored, and run out of conversation.

Be amusing without going over the top
It is not a good idea to flatter excessively or deliberately insult to make you appear clever, but on the other hand do try to show some spark of an interesting character.

Being dismissive or a people pleaser will rarely impress
Even if you think it is, avoid dismissing anything that the other person talks about as being trivial as you will

upset them and hurt their feelings. At the same time don't be a people pleaser and pander to everything they say in an obsequious way. A colleague of mine has a very annoying habit of making a statement about something and then when someone he wants to impress voices the opposite opinion, he immediately back tracks to fit in with them.

Keep a sense of humour

A sense of humour is essential. Everyone likes to laugh and it helps break down barriers and relaxes people. The ability to laugh and generate laughter in others is possibly one of the greatest attributes anyone could ever hope to acquire.

Be positive

Be positive in yourself and what you say. Try to imagine a positive outcome to this meeting and you will attract it like a magnet. A negative and complaining attitude is a complete turn off. Don't be someone who moans about others or pulls their ex to pieces. Try not to talk about your problems because everyone has enough of their own without needing yours to add to them.

Being too forceful can be a turn off

It's good to know what you want and to keep things moving, because you need to grab every opportunity to persuade your potential Date. However, try not to force your attentions on someone, because you might frighten them away if they feel they are being pressurised.

Interpreting Body Language

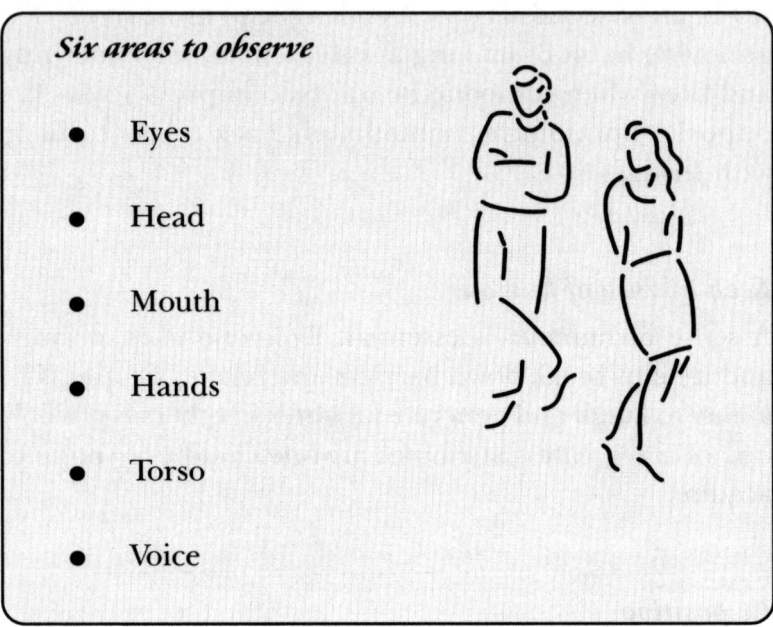

Six areas to observe

- Eyes
- Head
- Mouth
- Hands
- Torso
- Voice

Eyes

Eyes can reveal a great deal. The Victorians used to say that the eyes were *the mirror of your soul*. You may well be able to define whether a spark of chemistry has been generated by looking into the other person's eyes. Constant eye contact with you means that they are interested in what you are saying, and if they are gazing at you with admiration and don't seem to be in a hurry to leave you are doing well. Constantly looking you up and down is another positive sign. However, if you receive a glare, or the eyes are looking everywhere except at you, don't pin your hopes on this one. Also, eyes that appear to be drooping and falling asleep are a negative sign so be at your most awake and alert when out on your date.

Getting a Date

Head

A head held high with a bright facial expression probably indicates interest - someone who is interested in you will be alert and focused on what you are saying and doing. However, if their head starts rolling to one side or they give a vehement shake of the head to wake themselves up, things are definitely not going well, and it might be time to re-assess your conversational skills!

Mouth

A relaxed, wide and lasting smile is encouraging, whilst a frown is not. A quick tight smile every time the other person realises they have not been paying attention, or hidden yawns is less than encouraging. On the other hand if you receive an unexpected kiss you could be home and dry.

Hands

A limp handshake implies disinterest whilst a firm lingering handshake implies the opposite. Wringing of hands or excessive fidgeting implies a desperation to leave. Hands kept in pockets may demonstrate unwillingness for physical contact. Hands that keep touching you are a very encouraging sign.

Torso

If someone has an open stance, outstretched arms, they are open to your advances and are not protecting their body space. If they sit tightly with their arms crossed they are not relaxed and it will be difficult to get close to them. Someone who sits sideways on instead of facing you may be hiding part of themselves, and belongings such as a handbag or briefcase placed between you probably means a defence of their personal space. Fidgeting of any part of the torso and constant crossing of legs could indicate boredom. Of course if they walk away from you don't bother to follow.

Voice

The voice is very indicative of whether things are going well or not. Does it sound bored, or does it sound enthusiastic? Laughter is an excellent sign.

Asking for a Date

Once you feel that your potential is interested in you, asking for a date is not nearly as daunting a task as it may seem at first. Try not to be desperate that your invitation is accepted. Be relaxed without exerting any pressure.

Four suggested lines to ask for a date

- Would you fancy going out to dinner with me next week?

- Maybe we could have a drink sometime?

- May I use your pen? I'd like to give you my number and I hope you will call soon.

- I'd love to see you again. Would you like to see me?

Try to remember what interests or hobbies they have and suggest a date which will fit the bill.

Four suggested lines referring to interests

- Perhaps you would be interested in going out one night to see a film?

- I've been given a couple of tickets for .... concert/play on Saturday, would you like to come?

- Would you like to play tennis/golf etc. with me next ....?

- Let's go to this jive dance class I've been told about next week?

If you are not too sure of your ground or if you feel the other person is slightly nervous, a less threatening way of asking someone out on a date is to suggest a meeting with other people.

Four less threatening lines to ask for a date

- Would you and your friend like to meet up with me and some of my friends for a drink/at a club on Friday?

- Some friends have invited me to a dinner party next.... would you like to come with me?

- A bunch of us are going to.... would you like to come too?

- It's my birthday next...., and I'm having a party for friends. Would you like to come?

Remember that meeting a large number of your friends may be extremely daunting for your prospective Date. To encourage them to come along make the offer as informal as you can and suggest they bring along a friend or two so they won't feel intimidated by a whole bunch of new faces.

Finally, I must tell you about a very unusual and novel way one of my members gets his dates. He chats a girl up and then asks her to write her signature for him. He then says how interesting it is, and that he is into graphology and would like to do her signature analysis on his special computer programme. If she would like to give him her telephone number he will phone when the results are ready. Of course, once he has the results he phones and suggests they meet for dinner so that he can give her the analysis in person. It's one method which he has never known to fail!

Arranging the Date

Having achieved an agreement to go out on a date, try to make a firm commitment as to when this will be. Once you know when you are meeting, arrange what you are doing and where. Try to ascertain what your Date's preferences would be, but also give a few suggestions yourself. Try to suggest a public meeting place to give your Date a sense of security as they do not know you well enough yet. Try to avoid offering an invitation for a cosy night in at your place, and also avoid accepting such an invitation - it is too soon for the first date. If you have a favourite restaurant you know would be ideal, or have heard that a certain event has had rave revues, throw your ideas into the melting pot. When you have decided what the date will be, if you need time to organise tickets for the theatre/film or to book a restaurant, fix a time you can call (preferably the next day) to finalise arrangements. For women it is probably more acceptable to meet at the event. Once all the arrangements have been made, avoid any more contact such as phone calls until your meeting; it is best not to overwhelm. However, always make sure that you both have a contact number to ring at the last moment should anything untoward happen that might make you late for the date or unable to attend.

CHAPTER 4

THE FIRST DATE

(MAKING THE MOST OF IT!)

Congratulations! Now the hard bit's over, let's see how you can make the most of a great opportunity.

PREPARATION

You want to make sure you present yourself in the best possible light, so that if your Date turns out to be as promising as when you first met, you will be sure to secure a second date.

Four things to bear in mind preparing for the first date

- Good conversation topics

- Presentation

- Keeping calm

- Punctuality

Good conversation topics

Speaking from a lifetime of experience I have always found that if a person is right for you there will be no shortage of things to say. If you are both in tune, the time will pass so quickly that no date will ever be long enough to fit in all you want to say. If you struggle for something to talk about, this probably indicates you don't have much in common.

> **Three dates which do not require much conversation**
>
> - With friends
> - Going to a film/concert/play/opera/ballet
> - Playing a sport such as tennis/squash

With friends

If you have made a date where you will be going to meet friends at, for example, a dinner party, or even hosting the dinner party yourself, the situation will be much easier. You will feel more at ease having the moral support of others to introduce topics of conversation. If talking dries up between you, you can always include someone else into the disc,ussion.

Going to a film/concert/play/opera/ballet

Should you opt to see a film, conversation will be minimal. If you go to see a concert or to the theatre/opera/ballet, talking will be limited mainly to the interval. However with all these outings you have the advantage of being able to talk about a shared experience, whether you choose to enthuse or be critical.

Playing a sport such as tennis or squash

Perhaps your date is to play a sport and so conversation will be limited to referring to the score, or maybe praising your Date's performance and excusing your own.

Afterwards you will have lots to talk about as you dissect your game.

If the date you have chosen requires you to converse with each other most of the time, it may be advantageous to have a few topics of conversation up your sleeve. However I would not advise you to research your Date's occupation, hobby or interests. If you gain some superficial knowledge about a subject you can easily be caught out when it becomes apparent what you have done, and you could be made to feel foolish. For example, if your Date works for an oil company he/she might be flattered that you had learned the latest technology about drilling for oil in Trafalgar Square to impress. However, you might appear to be false and over keen at the same time, or maybe someone who just wants to say what others want to hear.

It is important to try to remember as much as you can about your first meeting, so that you can for example ask after their Great Aunt Fanny's trip to Disneyland; how they got on with their MOT; how their new job interview went. If they mentioned going to the cinema or musicals, find out all you can about the latest productions and releases so that if the opportunity arises you could suggest you both go and see one.

Read, watch and listen to as much as you can about current affairs in the media which will again give you topical subjects to discuss. Try not to count off the hours and the days until the date, but go out and do interesting things so that you have plenty of new experiences to talk about since you last met.

> **Five dates which require more conversation**
> - Dinner/lunch
> - Pub
> - Walk
> - Golf
> - Museum/exhibition

Dinner/lunch/pub

Going out to dinner/lunch or to the pub will give you ample opportunity to talk and get to know each other. Meeting for lunch is a great choice if you don't feel confident enough to spend an entire evening with your Date but still want to enjoy the intimate atmosphere and good conversation a meal can provide.

Walk/golf

Walking is a good way to see and get to know someone informally. If you choose the location carefully you will have plenty of good scenery to talk about. If your date is to play golf you will not only have the game to comment on, but plenty of time to talk as you hunt for lost balls!

Museum/exhibition

If either of you has a special interest in a particular subject then an appropriate museum or exhibition would be an ideal venue to converse at length on the subject.

Presentation

However nervous and ill at ease you may feel inside, your outward appearance must not show this. If you know you look your very best you will feel much more relaxed and confident, and this feeling will transmit to your Date and give them confidence in you. If you feel good, so will people around you.

Five things to bear in mind

- Face
- Hair
- Body
- Smell
- Clothes

Face

Make sure you have a few early nights before the date so that your eyes are sparkling as well as your personality. Also a clean, clear and fresh face is a must, so eat a healthy diet and drink plenty of water to avoid last minute skin eruptions. I think women should try not to wear heavy make-up but achieve a more natural look; after all if things go well, he will at some point see you without make-up and you wouldn't want to scare him with the stark contrast.

Hair

Make sure you have clean, shiny hair that looks very touchable; just the sort your Date would love to run their fingers through. Men with beards or moustaches would do well to trim them neatly, and those without, to make sure their face is stubble free. Women should also take care to keep any unwanted hair in check!

Body

Try to get some exercise into your schedule. You will feel more confident if you feel fit and toned up, and probably more attractive too.

Smell

Fresh, sweet smelling breath is a must, so give your teeth a good brushing. Strong smelling foods such as onions and garlic are best avoided before the date; alcohol, especially beer, will also give the breath an unmistakable smell. Of course if you accept an unexpected date shortly after having downed a pint of beer and a packet of cheese and onion crisps, emergency measures are necessary - be armed with mints or even a breath freshening spray.

Try to avoid overpowering aftershaves or perfumes. Your Date probably won't be as enamoured with your new scent and may even have an allergic reaction. I had a date years ago which was ruined because I was wearing a brand new perfume which I thought was great but dissolved my Date into such a paroxysm of sneezing he left me as soon as he felt he could.

Clothes

Make sure you know where you will be going and what you will be doing, so that you can dress appropriately for the occasion. If it is a surprise location then ask if you need formal or informal clothing. As a general rule it is always more acceptable to be casual and underdressed than overdressed. Overdressing can give the impression that you are trying too hard and make you seem less of a challenge, as well as making you feel somewhat out of place and awkward. Make sure your clothes and shoes are clean, and men please watch out for the gravy stains on your tie if you wear one.

If you think you look good, so will other people.

Keeping calm

A first date can be very daunting and nerve-racking and can reduce the strongest and coolest of us to a quivering blob of jelly. Anyone can panic when they are really keen on someone and want to make the best impression they can.

Here are a three simple things to bear in mind

- Give yourself enough time
- Think positively
- Be happy

Give yourself enough time

Allow yourself enough time to get ready so that you are not rushed, flustered and in a panic at the last moment. At the same time it is equally trying on the nerves to give yourself too much time to get ready. If you are ready too early you may spend the rest of the time pacing round worrying about your date, and whether your face, hair, clothes or body odour will have gone off the boil by the time you meet. I did this once and was eventually sick with nerves. I landed up having a second bath, a change of make-up and clothes at the last minute, and made myself late! Avoid all this by planning the hours before you meet like a military manoeuvre. If you don't rush yourself but also fill each minute with productive things to do, you will have less opportunity to worry. One tip I was taught is to drop your shoulders every time you get in a state - it's always worked for me!

Think positively

Thought-block all negative feelings about what will happen on the date and the outcome. Try to remember that you must have made a really good impression on your first meeting or you would not be embarking on this first date. Think positively that your Date will find you as likeable and attractive now as they obviously did the first time. I can't stress enough that if you always think of a positive scenario you will more often than not attract it like a magnet.

Be happy

Think happy thoughts, listen to happy music, watch a funny programme on TV, chat on the phone to a happy friend and *be happy*. Remember the most important thing you will wear is the expression on your face, and if you feel miserable with yourself so might your Date. However, if you present a happy welcoming expression you'll make your Date feel good and well disposed towards you. Try to remember that your Date is probably just as nervous as you are and just see the funny side of the situation - two people who are so keen to see each other that they decided to make a date, but who are petrified about this meeting and worried sick that the other won't still like them.

Punctuality

It shows good manners, a thoughtful caring personality, and respect for the other person to be on time.

Two things to bear in mind

- Think ahead

- Be good humoured

Think ahead

Always think ahead and allow time for possible delays. For example if you are driving, listen to traffic reports to see if there are any jams along the way; also allow time to get lost and find a parking space. If you are going by public transport make sure there are no strikes in progress and listen to the radio for news of any other delays. If you are late, tell the truth about the reason why. This will be far more endearing and give you more credibility than if you had made up an excuse. A few simple words such as 'I've got no excuse, I just didn't allow myself enough time to drive here', or 'Halfway here I realised that I'd left your address at home', will suffice.

Be good humoured

If your Date turns up late, be good humoured and laid back about it; at least they turned up! Let them see that you are a good natured and reasonable person, and you will win quite a few Brownie points.

HOW TO HANDLE THE DATE

Think of the date as several separate sections.

The five sections of a first date

- Greeting

- Relaxing

- Probing

- Hook

- Closure and Clinch

Greeting

You meet; what do you do next? In many countries, and in many social circles a kiss on both cheeks would be appropriate. However, if you feel unsure of your ground and don't want to seem overly familiar, shaking hands warmly is least likely to offend. At the same time make sure you have a warm welcoming smile and say something simple like 'It's good to see you again. How was your journey?' The greeting section is just general stress-free chit chat about, for example, the weather; how did they get there; how nice they look etc. It is good therapy to start the conversation with topics you don't have to think about, because you are both adjusting to the environment and need time to feel relaxed with each other. Don't launch straight into a thinking topic such as politics or a serious social issue as you'll appear awkward and intense and will probably throw your Date off balance. It is best to give each other space to relax with non threatening conversation.

Try to bear in mind your own body language such as constant eye contact; an open stance; a wide lasting smile; an enthusiastic voice; and remember to listen intently without fidgeting. When you feel more confident move to the next section - relaxing.

Relaxing

Anything you can remember about your Date from your first meeting comes into play here. Ask them about their new job or their forthcoming holiday plans. Show that you have paid them some attention, but be careful not to labour over details. Be prepared to branch out spontaneously and talk about whatever comes to mind and remember that there's a fine line between a keen interest and an obsession.

Try to introduce some humour into the conversation, because helping your Date to laugh will make them feel good and therefore even better disposed towards you. You could even carry around a joke gadget as an attention-sparker when conversation needs perking up! Seeing the ridiculous and absurd in almost any situation is one of the most priceless gifts of all. Sir Winston Churchill once said 'It is my belief, you cannot deal with the most serious things in the world unless you understand the most amusing.' How right he was.

Always try to remember to be positive at all times in whatever you say, and avoid moaning or complaining about anyone or anything because that is tedious and off-putting to listen to.

Probing

This is when you will start to find out about the other person and whether there is any mutual compatibility; this is an important learning time for both of you. Ask if they prefer winter holidays such as skiing to a summer holiday basking in the sun; find out if they are very active and like to run ten miles before breakfast or whether they prefer to lie in bed reading a book or cuddling their pet python; whether they are a strict vegetarian who objects to others eating animal flesh; whether they might be teetotal or alcoholic; whether they are racist; whether they are very religious or strongly atheist; whether they are early risers or night owls; whether they are fiercely tidy or prefer to live in a mess; whether they are ambitious or content with what they have.

If there is anything you feel is important to find out about the other, this is the time to do it; it is better that you find out something now, which would be intolerable for you to live with, rather than later.

However, I must stress here that there is no such person as a perfect person. Be flexible, and try not to have too many fixed ideas as to what you are searching for, because this can eventually keep you on the side-lines of life and prevent you from enjoying potentially pleasurable and promising relationships. In fact if you have always gone out with a particular type and those relationships have never worked out, maybe it is time to change your pattern and be less rigid in your requirements.

If your Date asks you probing questions, resist the temptation to talk about yourself for too long, which could become boring. Also try not to show off about your exploits or boast about your achievements; you will gain far more brownie points by being modest and understated.

Hook

If you are still as keen as ever and want to catch your fish, you could try some of the following bait.

> *Seven ways to keep HIM on the hook*
>
> - Be yourself and try not to copy anyone else
> - Be attentive and enthusiastic
> - Win his trust, build his confidence and flatter
> - Show appreciation of his jokes
> - Be warm and inviting but maintain a distance
> - Be trouble free, relaxed and fun to be with
> - Leave him wanting more of you

Be yourself and try not to copy anyone else

If you can't be yourself then there is no point in going any further. Any pretences won't last and no-one appreciates their girlfriend turning out to be a phoney.

Be attentive and enthusiastic

Use lots of body language such as eye contact, leaning forward, and enthusiastic nods and comments. Listen and encourage him to tell you about himself, and let him know how fascinated you are.

Win his trust, build his confidence and flatter

Let him know that you are just happy to be with him and you don't want anything else from him. A man could be easily frightened away if he thought you were looking for a meal ticket so let him feel that he would be safe and understood with you. Focus on any positive similarities you may have, and also make some intelligent observations which will demonstrate and give him confidence that you have brains as well as beauty. Ask him questions about something he is very knowledgeable about, and let him know how much he has enlightened you; make him feel important. In all he tells you about himself and his life, show that you only see the best in him. If you see or hear something about him that you genuinely admire, then flatter him for all you are worth - flattery will help get you everywhere!

Show appreciation of his jokes

Laugh at his jokes and witty comments and show him how entertaining you find him to be. Let him see how impressed you are with his sense of humour, and that you are both on the same wavelength with a lot in common. However, remember that your laughter will be most effective in making him feel good and appreciated if it's used *occasionally* - so be sure to laugh only when he's being genuinely witty.

Be warm and inviting but maintain a distance

Wear some sexy underwear that will make *you* feel desirable and mysterious. Wear clothes that accentuate just enough of your best assets (legs, bust, right elbow etc.) to whet his appetite. Occasionally and unthinkingly touch his arm, rest your hand fleetingly on his knee, or brush a hair off his jacket to let him hope and think he could be in with a chance *but* keep a hidden barrier which says *you can look, you can touch/kiss if I let you, but you can only go so far!*

Be trouble free, relaxed and fun to be with

Let him know you are happy with your life. Don't mention your problems and never moan or complain or nag - men can't stand it. Let him feel that life with you would be comfortable and hassle free, and not a life sentence of exhaustively trying to keep up with you. On the other hand indicate that life with you would be fun and not a drag, and always try to accentuate the positive in everything.

Leave him wanting more of you

Try not to give your all, but maybe keep about 30% of yourself and your life history back for future dates. Let him think there is a lot more of interest to get to know about you. Do what every great theatrical performer does - leave your audience wanting more.

Seven ways to keep HER on the hook

- Be attentive and romantic
- Keep her guessing as to your availability
- Try not to be too keen
- Be relaxed and confident
- Indicate ambition and knowledge
- Show a little vulnerability
- Leave her wanting more

Be attentive and romantic

In general women (unless they are dedicated to feminism) like men to be attentive towards them. Show you have a caring personality and good manners. Pay her compliments and tell her how lovely she is looking; how much you like her perfume; how much you admire her outfit - but don't overdo it. Compliments should sound discerning and sensitive and not obligatory and insincere.

Most women would go for a romantic man; just look at the way they idolise romantic heroes in films. Romance can be shown easily by choosing a romantic situation such as a candle lit supper for two, a moonlit walk holding hands, or a small gift of flowers. Any gesture which indicates that you are not just Macho but also have romance in your soul will stand you in good stead.

Keep her guessing as to your availability

Imply that you are not totally available by feeding subtle clues that not all your nights are free. Mention recent places you have gone for dinner, or current plays/shows/films you have seen, and leave her wondering who you took to see them and whether she has competition. Many women are turned on by a challenge.

Try not to be too keen

By all means pay her compliments but don't go overboard and shower her with them. Let her know you are interested, but try not to let slip that you have thought of and talked about no one else since you last met. Keep her guessing, and never appear to be desperate; most women don't want a pushover.

Be relaxed and confident

Be relaxed and confident in yourself and show that you are someone who is happy with what he has. For example by slowly standing up to greet her rather then jumping to your feet; by calling the waiter over to take her coat, you show self assurance and a casual manner which will put her at her ease straight away. Women, in general, like to feel that their man is dependable, poised and strong.

Indicate ambition and knowledge

Indicate that although you are someone who is happy with your lot in life, you have goals you aspire to and are always striving to increase your knowledge and skills. For example, you can announce your intention to learn a foreign language before going on holiday this year, or that you are attending a training course which will help you to secure promotion in your job. Let her see you have prospects and are moving places.

Talk about something which interests you, especially if it is fascinating. For example an interest in current affairs: there's always plenty of stimulating news stories which merit discussion. Show that you have an inquisitive mind and are aware of what is going on around you. However, be careful not to sound rehearsed and pompous. Indicate that you like your life to be interesting and fun. Be spontaneous and remember that most women want a man with imagination.

Show a little vulnerability

Although it is good to show that you have inner strength, it is also important to let her know that you are not an island but you also need help and advice. Genuinely show that you value her judgement and reveal your more vulnerable side.

Leave her wanting more
As I have recommended to women, keep about 30% of yourself and your life unrevealed. Keep her interested, intrigued and keen to see you again to get to know more about you.

Closure and Clinch

One of the thoughts that may be drifting through your mind at this point might be *who pays?* In general the person who issued the invitation usually pays the bill, however, if you feel more comfortable offering to pay half it would always be appreciated, even if your offer is not accepted. Any woman going out with a man she knows nothing at all about, might be well advised to pay her half share in order to avoid any misunderstandings about implied obligations. One of my friends has a really gallant way of asking a woman out, he says 'You chose and book the restaurant, I'll pay the bill.' In this way she feels she has contributed to the evening by having the responsibility of booking the right venue, and he is happy to foot the bill!

It is better to end the date too soon and leave you both wanting more of each other's company, than to exhaust the conversation. You will also be more likely to receive an invitation for a second date if he/she is disappointed that this one has gone by so quickly. It is always better to take a new relationship slowly; very often relationships that start quickly end in the same way. The same goes for sex; it is better to end the first date with a peck on the cheek rather than a heavy petting session or rushing straight to bed; if you take things slowly you might inspire a lot more passion and respect.

In general, serious relationships do not blossom from one night stands. If you are out together on a weekday evening you could for example look at your watch and say 'I had no idea that the time has gone by so fast. I really don't want to, but I'll have to go. Maybe we could meet again soon and carry on where we left off?'

If the answer is favourable then make an arrangement to call the next day to arrange the second date. Of course, if you want to make your date even more keen don't hint at when the next meeting might be; say your good-byes and keep them guessing. If the reply is luke warm then maybe they are not so keen as you so don't push the subject, say your good-byes and leave. Should you be asked back to their place for a coffee don't necessarily assume that this means you are being asked to stay the night. Assume it's for coffee, and if you do go, leave after about an hour. If you want to stay the night, then at this stage if the feeling is mutual, I'm sure you will be asked. However, I must reiterate that holding back on the first date will make a second more likely and much more exciting!

What if things go wrong?

If the rendezvous doesn't go according to plan and your feelings for your Date (or their feelings towards you) have changed, it's really not the end of the world. Remember that this was an exploratory meeting which could have gone either way, and this person was by no means your last hope for happiness; there are plenty more fish in the sea.

If you feel uncomfortable, then don't subject yourself to any more than you have to. Make your excuses and leave. If your meeting is during the day then cutting the date short is fairly easy. Your Date will accept that you may be busy and have things do, so leave as soon as you have made your excuses. If things go wrong at night you could leave because you're not feeling well or because you have to be at work early in the morning. If you have doubts about your Date, then if you have a mobile phone, arrange for a friend to call you at a specific time giving you an excuse to leave if you need it. However, do be aware that many people find mobile phones intrusive, especially on a date! But, to be honest, if things are going so horribly wrong that you want to leave, any excuse will do.

Please don't despair if the date was awful. Most people, if you can get them to admit it, have been through some strange or upsetting times during their dating career, and yours will by no means be unique. In fact I have been told about so many bizarre dating experiences that I felt they warranted a chapter on their own. So please read on in Chapter 5 about some *Dates from Hell!*

CHAPTER 5

DATES FROM HELL!
(YOU ARE NOT ALONE!)

A Heated Discussion

John and Brian met with Sue and Jane at the pub and asked them out to dinner. Another friend, Graham, was with them, and as they had previously arranged to go out with him, they agreed to drop him off at his place before taking the girls out. Off they set in the car with Brian and Graham sitting in front, and John and the two girls squeezed in the back. John was sitting next to Jane, the girl he fancied, and she was wearing a beautiful long silk scarf. Putting his right arm round her shoulders he lit up his cigarette with his left hand and everything was cosy for a while. After a few minutes Brian said he was sure he could smell burning and opened his window to see if the smell was coming from outside. Suddenly there was a shriek from the back as Jane looked down at her scarf and realised she was on fire. They managed to save her, but the scarf was ruined and so was the date; John was given a load of abuse from Jane, and also eventually from Brian as Sue sided with Jane and the two girls stomped off. The only person left laughing was Graham!

Drowned off!

I once went out to dinner on a first date to a very exclusive restaurant in London. We ordered the meal and an extremely expensive bottle of red wine; we chatted away and the evening was going well. The wine was brought to the table, our glasses were filled, and as we toasted each other I made an elaborate gesture with my other hand and spilt the rest of the bottle all over him and his impressive looking suit. Strangely enough he never asked me out again.

Journey to Hell!

A friend of mine, Alec, was working in Germany and met a Swiss girl called Brigitta one night in a hotel bar. By the end of the evening they were getting on really well, but unfortunately she was going back to Switzerland the next day. They exchanged telephone numbers and promised to call each other. Over the next few weeks they spoke a lot on the phone and one day she asked him to spend the next weekend at her place in Vaduz, Switzerland. As you can imagine my friend was overjoyed at the prospect of a weekend with her; he bought his plane ticket, re-arranged business appointments so that he could take the Friday and Monday off, and spent the remaining days and nights working to make sure nothing would be left undone. Full of excited anticipation he set off on the Friday morning to see her.

He arrived at Zurich airport and then took a train up into the mountains to Vaduz. When he arrived at his destination she was there to greet him, but she wasn't alone. Apparently while she was waiting for him to arrive she had bumped into an ex-boyfriend, Jochem, and they had got chatting. She now suggested that all three of them go off for drinks and lunch. After lunch she said they were going to her apartment and Jochem came too. They chatted all afternoon and Alec was beginning to get fed up with the situation, but couldn't get an opportunity to speak to Brigitta on her own. By early evening she said she was hungry, and suggested that they all go out for dinner. By the end of the evening Alec was completely bewildered, and when they eventually got back to her place, he was given the couch and she and Jochem went to her bedroom.

As you can imagine, Alec didn't sleep a wink all night, and as soon as morning came he left whilst they were still sleeping. He got a taxi to the station, a train to Zurich and waited for the first flight home. A truly awful date from hell!

Given the Boot

Sara, who lived in London, was invited out on a first date to fly to Paris for dinner. She was so thrilled she bought a new outfit and some very fashionable new boots. When they arrived in Paris he said he'd like them to wander around town before dinner and she readily agreed. Just before all the shops closed, she caught the heel of her new boot in the pavement and it snapped in half. It was too late to get any kind of footwear and they had dinner booked at one of the most exclusive restaurants in Paris. She had to hobble along into the restaurant, and whilst many men would have seen the funny side of the situation, he didn't. It was a somewhat frosty dinner and she felt mortified; by the time they arrived back at Heathrow she knew they wouldn't be dining together or even seeing each other again!

A Deadly Reply

Anthony was out on his first date with a nurse called Rosemary whom was very keen on. They were driving along when he saw a Skoda car coming towards them, and seeking to impress her with his knowledge on cars he said 'Have you heard all the Skoda jokes? How do you double the value of a Skoda? – Fill up the fuel tank! – They're terrible cars, just like the Lada, badly manufactured and can be a very poor investment.'

'I'm sorry you said that,' she replied 'my father saved up every penny he could to buy a Lada as it was the only new car he could afford.' There was an awkward silence; he realised he had to say something to save the situation and wanted to show that he wasn't spineless. 'I stand by what I said but I didn't mean to offend your father. I'd love to meet him so we could discuss the pros and cons of his car. When's he free?' he said. 'My father died two months ago' was the reply.

A Merry Dance

James knew that Annette loved the opera and he decided that a good way to win her affections would be to take her on a date to see one at The Royal Opera House in London. He bought the tickets and told her that he had a surprise date for her. They met early evening in Covent Garden and he took her for a meal. During dinner he intimated that he also was an opera fan and knew quite a lot about the subject and that their date tonight was to see the opera *Romeo and Juliet* at the Royal Opera House. She was thrilled, especially since this was the first time she had heard of this opera.

They arrived at The Opera House, he bought the programmes, they sat in their seats and then as he opened his programme the awful truth dawned upon him – *Romeo and Juliet* was a ballet! They sat through two hours of a ballet in which neither of them was interested and she fell asleep!

Man of her Nightmares?

Christine had been invited out for dinner by the most handsome, well mannered and well dressed man she had ever met in her life. This was truly the man of her dreams. She got herself ready and sat waiting in her flat with eager anticipation for the doorbell to ring, and for her date of a lifetime to begin. The bell rang and she opened the door. She was somewhat surprised when she saw him standing there unshaven, smelling of drink, dressed in scruffy jeans, and then horrified as he rushed in, threw her to the floor and landed on top of her. 'Most men **** their woman after they've bought them dinner. I do it the other way round!' he said. 'Not with me you don't!' she retorted and threw him out of her flat.

Love Story with a Difference

Jenny was a shy girl whom Andrew thought the world of and wanted to get to know better. He decided to take her to a cinema in Cardiff to see *Love Story*, which had just been released. As they stood in the crowded foyer however, Andrew realised that the tickets were sold out. Suddenly an attendant announced 'Two spare tickets for upstairs!'. Andrew jumped at the chance, grabbed Jenny's hand, paid the attendant, and they took their seats.

Andrew looked around the cinema and began to experience a vague sense of alarm when he saw the audience consisted entirely of men. The credits went up and he felt even more dismay when the film began. The opening scene was a scantily clad woman who walked into the room, peeled all her clothes off and knelt down in front of an equally scantily dressed man. At this stage Andrew turned to the man on his left and said in a loud voice 'Is this *Love Story?*' No mate' was the reply, 'This is....' The whole cinema erupted into laughter because this was a particularly steamy film as different from *Love Story* as chalk from cheese. The lewd remarks directed towards Jenny as they walked out of the cinema sealed Andrew's fate.

Hell Hath No Fury Like Annie Scorned!

Annie had lusted after Harry for months and finally he asked her out for dinner the next Saturday. She was beside herself with excitement and immediately went out to buy a new outfit for the occasion and made bookings at the hairdresser, and to have a facial on Saturday morning. The great day arrived, and just as she got home from her beauty treatments, the telephone rang - it was Harry, who said he was really sorry he would have to cancel their date. He'd had an accident playing squash the day before and had spent all night in Casualty with an injured shoulder. It was very painful and he had an appointment with the physiotherapist that evening, then he was going to bed. However, he would call her next week to arrange another date.

Annie was obviously very disappointed, but wished him well and said she'd look forward to hearing from him. Later that evening she phoned him to make sure he was OK but there was no answer. He must have unplugged the phone, she thought. Next day, she met some friends in the pub, and couldn't believe her ears when someone mentioned they had seen Harry walking into a restaurant with a new leggy blonde the previous night.

On Monday, Annie phoned Harry and very sweetly asked how he was feeling and said she felt so sorry for him that she would love to take him out on Wednesday night to cheer him up. Harry couldn't believe his luck and readily accepted. She said she knew a beautiful old pub quite far away set in glorious countryside and would pick him up in her car and drive him there.

Wednesday came and after a two hour drive they arrived at the wonderful pub seemingly far from civilisation. They sat down and she insisted on buying the drinks because she didn't want him to exert himself too much after his awful accident. In fact, she bought the second round and even insisted on buying the third - off she went to the bar and Harry was impressed. After half an hour he wondered where she had got to and went to find her. He couldn't see her anywhere, she wasn't at the bar and so he asked the barmaid if she would look in the Ladies to see if Annie was alright.

When the barmaid came back and told him the Ladies was empty the awful truth dawned on Harry. He had been dumped a two hour drive away from home in the middle of nowhere with no means of transport! When he finally managed to persuade a local taxi firm to drive him back at enormous cost, he furiously gave directions to Annie's flat. As he got out of the taxi he heard her voice calling him from an upstairs window, and looking up he saw her smiling and drinking champagne. 'Bye, bye Harry,' she called, and shut the window.

Dates from Hell!

Mistaken Identity

Laura was recovering from a messy divorce and decided she was ready to start dating again. She had always found it amusing to scour the personal columns in her daily newspaper, but now she decided to answer some of the adverts herself. A few days later she had a call from Peter, one of the advertisers, who suggested they should meet up the next night. They arranged to meet on the platform of her local railway station, and he said he would be carrying a rolled umbrella. She arrived on the platform early so as to be sure not to miss him, and looking around she saw a real hunk carrying a rolled umbrella. She couldn't believe her luck! She went up to him and said, 'Hi, I'm Laura,' and started chatting to him. After a while she suggested that they go off somewhere together and was surprised when he called his friends over. It took quite a time at the local police station to convince these plain clothes police officers that she was not the woman there had been recent complaints about for soliciting unsuspecting rail travellers!

Woof, woof!

Ruth was a good-natured girl who loved doing things for others, until she met Joe. Joe was very good looking and knew it. Every girl he had ever met couldn't do enough for him. He was also quite tight with his money when it came to girlfriends; since he'd started going out with Ruth, three months ago, he had never bought her meal. In fact, he demanded food from her at a moment's notice at any time of the day or night, complaining if it took too long to prepare and never giving her any thanks.

One day Ruth's patience ran out, and she rang him up to ask him over that night to share a delicious stew she had just made. Later she served him his food but said she felt unwell and couldn't face anything to eat. He tucked in and for once in his life said how delicious the meal was, and asked for more. After the third helping, he contentedly sat back and enquired what she had put in this delicious stew. 'Just four cans of ....dog food!' she said. Needless to say he never demanded another meal from her again.

CHAPTER 6

THE SECOND DATE

(THE FOLLOW UP, PREPARATION AND PERFORMANCE)

THE FOLLOW UP

The first date is over and perhaps you had a good time, but do you really want a second date? To discover your true feelings you need to take time to evaluate what's happened so far.

Evaluating the first date

Is there any chemistry between you? There may be one or many of the following issues to take into consideration and you may well think of more.

Six factors to take into consideration

- Attraction

- Common interests

- Lifestyle

- Friends

- Distance

- Mutual attraction

Attraction
Questions to ask yourself....

Do you spend much of your time thinking and dreaming about them, does your heart flip, your pulse race and do you feel a glow when you do so?

Can you still imagine their touch and smell and does it please you?

Do you long to be with them, and do your fingers itch every time you are near a phone, to call them?

Did you like their body shape, hair, eyes, mouth, smile, voice, the way they dressed and moved? Did you in fact like them?

Was there anything in what they said about themselves, others, or general topics that surprised, disappointed or maybe took you aback?

Would you like them as a friend and confidant?

Do you feel you could really be yourself (warts and all) with them, or would you be anxiously watching your words and actions in case you should displease?

Did you find them interesting, stimulating and fun?

Most importantly - did you feel comfortable?

Common interests
Questions to ask yourself....

Do you have the same tastes in, for example, music, TV programmes, food and drink, holidays, newspapers?

Can you imagine sharing your leisure pursuits with them such as tennis/golf/sailing or watching football/wrestling; going to the theatre/concerts/opera/ballet; going out to dinner/to the pub/to the disco; bee keeping/bell ringing/taxidermy/brass rubbing; walking in the countryside or mountain climbing; visiting museums; travel and sightseeing?

Would you have enough common interests to make life interesting and fun, or do you think it could sink into dull routine?

Do you have vastly differing political views?

Are your body clocks the same; does one of you like to stay up late whilst the other prefers early to bed/early to rise?

Were you excited that you had similar views and ideas, or unexpected coincidences of doing/saying the same thing at the same time?

Would you say you were on the same mental wavelength and have a similar sense of humour?

Did you make each other laugh?

Did you have any clashes of views resulting in a heated discussion?

Would you say you have similar temperaments?

If not, could you cope with their different nature, or would it irritate or upset you?

Lifestyle
Questions to ask yourself....

Would they fit into your lifestyle or could you fit into theirs?

Do they for example live a somewhat bohemian lifestyle whilst yours is very ordered and traditional?

Are you ambitious to achieve new goals and improve your lifestyle whilst they are content to stay with their lot, and would feel uncomfortable moving up the ladder?

Maybe you live in a castle and they live in a shack. Could you spend time in each other's home and do you think there could be a comfortable compromise?

Do you come from similar backgrounds or is there a wide social gap between you?

Are you a homely type who likes pottering around the house, whilst they never eat in and are always out socialising?

Friends
Questions to ask yourself....

From what you have heard about or been able to observe of their friends, would you want to spend time with them?

Are they your kind of people?

We can all be influenced by friends to a great extent. A business colleague of mine started going out with a man who was wonderful company and generally displayed moderation in all things. Everything was great until she met his friends. Their idea of a good evening out was to go to the pub and have really heavy drinking sessions. As their relationship continued she was expected to spend night after night in the pub with him. Eventually the drinking ruined their relationship and she had to tell him that she couldn't continue. Afterwards she told me what a pity it was, because whilst they were on their own they used to have a great time, but all the time they spent with friends gradually became intolerable. This is a classic case of someone's friends ruining a relationship. Therefore other people's friends should always be taken into consideration when thinking about entering into a relationship with them.

Distance
I'm sure that lust at first sight exists, but surveys have shown that true love at first sight is just knowledge after the initial get together. Therefore if they live a long distance away

from you, do you have enough time and energy to travel to gain that knowledge? Are you ready to go, regularly, to a lot of trouble and hassle just to see them, and is it worth putting your work and health in jeopardy by maybe tiring yourself out in the process? Would you eventually be willing to move to their area?

Mutual attraction
Questions to ask yourself....

A very important factor is what you think was their impression of you. Do you think they felt any chemistry between you?

Do you think that the conversation gelled or was it hard work? Did your jokes fall flat?

Did their body language indicate that they were bored and unimpressed with you?

Did they leave early with an unexpected excuse?

The Good Dating Guide

Getting the Second Date

Having taken all these factors into account do you still want to go ahead? If the answer is yes; you genuinely like them; feel you could be compatible; think you could have fun together; feel that this liaison could be worth your time and effort; then you need to plan your next step. I feel I must reiterate here that the myth that women never and shouldn't make the first move is out of date. If you are a woman and strongly feel you want to contact a man, then do it and show your confidence. He'll probably be extremely flattered.

When to try

You don't want to appear over enthusiastic, but on the other hand you don't want to appear to be disinterested. It is the nature of how you handle the contact rather than the timing which is important. You can make contact the next day if you feel so inclined, but what you say must be just friendly and unpressured. Maybe just saying thank you for a great time out together would be unlikely to cause offence.

How to make contact

Four options to try

- Call
- Send flowers
- Write
- Accidental meeting

Call

If you decide that although you are keen you suspect the feeling is not mutual, probably the best thing to do is not to chase after them; you could risk making a nuisance of yourself and cause embarrassment. Try to think of your situation as being like an elastic band between you. The more you go towards them the slacker the tension becomes and the further they can move away. The more you move away the tighter the tension becomes and the more you pull them towards you. The safest thing to do whether your feelings are reciprocated or not, is to call and say thank you for the good time you had together; ask how they are and whether they had a good journey back (if you didn't escort them home) and briefly converse in a general way. They will have had time to reflect on your first date, and you will probably be able to gauge from their response and tone of voice whether your attentions are welcome.

If they seem cool, then end the conversation with something like 'Well, I must go now, I should have met a friend 5 minutes ago. I'm glad you got back alright; it was good speaking to you. Have a great day. Bye.'

When you have put the phone down don't jump to conclusions such as they can't stand the sight of you. There could be many reasons for their apparent disinterest. Maybe they are at work and in the middle of a business meeting; maybe they just jumped out of the bath to answer the phone, tripped on the bath mat and were lying, freezing cold, on the floor in a puddle of water; maybe they had just spilt coffee in their computer; maybe the TV had blown up', nothing is impossible. Just calm yourself down and decide to call again in a few days as a last ditch attempt.

When you call again say something like, 'I can't get you out of my mind, and I would like to invite you out to dinner whenever you can make it. If you can't make an arrangement now, please give me a call whenever you like. I'd love to hear from you.' You've now left the ball in their court; don't wait around for the phone call but keep busy, go out and leave the ansaphone on. If they are not interested they won't call.

Try to imagine why they could have been disappointed in you. Did you lean across and give them an unwelcome surprise kiss? Did you unwittingly embarrass or insult them? Did you talk too much about yourself? Were you too nervous and quiet? Bear in mind anything you think of and be careful to avoid it on your next first date.

However remember, that if you cannot be yourself with someone, then that person is the wrong someone for you. Don't feel depressed, just do as the song says: *'pick yourself up, dust yourself down and start all over again.'*

If on the other hand the response on the first call is enthusiastic; after you have asked if they got back safely and generally chatted, you could end the conversation by saying something like 'Well I must go now, I just wanted to say thank you and check you were OK. Maybe I could call again soon? When would be convenient for you?' Agree to phone at the convenient time, hang up and give yourself a pat on the back.

Send flowers

Sending flowers is a very pleasant way to follow up a date. Traditionally it is men who do this but there is no reason why a woman shouldn't do the same. I think that a leafy green plant that he could put either in his home or office would be a splendid gesture, and one which would surprise and flatter him. It really doesn't matter who they are, a surprise gift will be appreciated by anybody. With your flowers put a message such as *Thank you for a lovely time. I really enjoyed myself and hope you did too. Best wishes.*

You will almost certainly get a response, even if it is simply to thank you for your gift. If you receive a phone call, say how much you enjoyed the date and how you would like to repeat it. If the response is enthusiastic then clinch the deal. If the response is luke warm say, for example 'Give me a call whenever you like if you find you have a free moment and would like to go out somewhere.' The onus is then on them to make the next move, and if they are keen they will; however, mentally I think you should move on.

Write

Send a note the next day thanking them for a great time and to say how much you enjoyed their company. Say you do hope you can meet up again soon. If you don't hear back within a week give them a call. Say how you would love to see them again and that you would like to invite them out for perhaps a drink. If the response is good make your arrangements; if it is not, proceed as mentioned in the above two paragraphs.

Accidental meeting

You could wait for a few days to see if they contact you, and if you don't hear anything plan an accidental meeting. If you have mutual friends, try to find out your Date's movements and coincidentally bump into them. If you know where they work, or where they have their lunch break, again bump into them by accident. After the collision say something like 'What a lovely surprise, how are you. I thought the film we saw last week was brilliant, thank you so much for taking me. Maybe you'd like to have dinner with me some time?' If they mumble excuses and look embarrassed, quickly say 'Well I must dash. Great to see you, give me a call sometime' and mentally get back to the drawing board (their loss, not yours). If the response is good, say for example 'Great, when can I give you a call to arrange a date?' Mentally give yourself a standing ovation and ring at the appointed time.

What should the second date be?

As the first date went so well, you could take the safe option of repeating what you did before but maybe in a different location; for example a different restaurant, wine bar, film/play etc. However, you now know a lot more about them and about what they enjoy doing, so you could suggest something different. Try to remember if there was a particular film or concert they wanted to see; a restaurant they had heard was good; if they had always wanted to fly in a microlight plane; if they like long walks; line dancing; looking round art galleries; going hot air ballooning; clay pigeon shooting. Anything that you think might please and delight them would be a good choice to suggest. If you opted for a first date where you had little time to talk to each other such as going to a film, or out with friends, maybe you could make sure you have plenty of time to chat and really get to know each other on the second.

PREPARATION

Let's take stock of the situation. You have evaluated the first date and remembered all you could about their character, views, pursuits and lifestyle and decided that there could be the basis of a good relationship. Of course much of what we discussed in Chapter 3 on preparing for the first date applies to preparation for the second. For example making sure you look your best; leaving yourself the right amount of time to get ready; steadying your nerves; being on time; not being upset if they are late. However what more should we consider on preparing for the second date?

Three things to take into consideration

- What more should you find out about him/her?

- What more should you reveal of your true self?

- What should you expect sexually?

What more should you find out about him/her?

If there were any particular interests you share which please you, then say so. For example, if you shared a good meal together, you could say 'I'm so pleased you like going out to dinner and enjoy your food. So many people are fussy about what they eat that eating out is not a pleasure. I really enjoy dining out and I'm so glad we share the same interest.'

If they reply enthusiastically that they are delighted too, you can start to mention other similarities which make you happy. For example, 'I'm so pleased that you like going for long walks, so many people just like walking to the pub,' or 'I was so pleased to hear you like going to the theatre/opera; most of my friends just like going to the cinema'.

Having discussed things that you like about each other, you may well be able to start asking more searching questions. If you are to have a relationship you will need to feel comfortable enough to discuss almost anything at length with one another. You now need to seek avenues to discover more about them and their feelings for you. Your questions should be sufficiently general; not necessarily requesting intimate details of the other's life but just sufficient to gauge if they would like to take the relationship further.

Four avenues to explore

- Career

- Friends

- Family

- Personal needs

Career

Your questions need to show a natural interest and should not appear to be prying. For example, you could ask how long they have been in their job and whether they intend to stay with their company and work their way to executive level, or do they want to move from industry to industry to build up an impressive CV. If they give a detailed reply, this could mean that they are happy giving personal information to you and might be an indication of how they feel about you.

Friends

Maybe you can find out whether you have any competition; if they are going out with anyone else at present. You could tactfully try to find out whether they are seeing anyone else by jokingly saying, 'I hope you're not going out with a 7ft Judo expert who's going to walk in here and give me a black eye,' or 'I hope you're not seeing anyone like that woman in *Fatal Attraction.*' If they evade the question maybe there is someone else, or maybe they don't feel comfortable with you. Are they playing games with you or do they intend to be serious?

Family

You could try to find out more about their parents - whether they are still alive, still married, live near, or whether they go to visit them very much. You can learn a lot about someone from the way they discuss their parents; you may gather how their parents influenced them, and whether they have a caring close relationship. Try to also find out about their relationship with siblings if they have any. Answers to all these questions will help to build up a picture of your Date's inner self and what influenced their development.

You will also need to know if they have children of their own, and whether the children live with them and take up the majority of their time. Their children could have a great influence on your relationship and you need to know the score as soon as possible. Would you be ready to take on the responsibility of someone else's children?

Personal needs

Try to subtly find out what your Date's personal needs are. Are they just looking for a good time; a serious relationship leading to cohabitation; a serious relationship leading to marriage; a means by which they could give up work and be a person of leisure; someone to give them children; someone to be a devoted slave? It is best to find out at an early stage rather than get hurt later on. But remember that these are big subjects to deal with, so they must be approached in a careful and sensitive manner.

Find out if their hobby or any other interest is very time consuming, and does it rule their lives. For example do they play golf all weekend to the exclusion of everything else? If you don't play you could land up being a golf widow/widower, unless you fancy being a reluctant caddie on a windswept golf course and propping up the bar to discuss the game afterwards.

It is good advice to try to spot incompatibility at an early stage as this could help avoid a lot of heartache later.

What more should you reveal of your true self?

Anything that you feel is important to you and your own personal well being should be mentioned.

> ***Four areas to consider revealing more about***
>
> - Career
> - Friends
> - Family
> - Personal needs

Career

If you are ambitious and it is important for you to move up the career ladder, you need to make your feelings known. It may be that your work takes you away a lot or that you want to work abroad at some point. All this is important information that needs to be imparted to avoid misunderstandings at a later stage. Again though, it is a big topic and will need careful discussion with your new partner. If you are not ambitious and would not appreciate being left on your own for long periods of time, you would be well advised to intimate this.

Friends

If your friends are an important part of your life and you need to spend time with them, then tell your Date all about them and what you get up to. Try to gauge their reactions and whether they would like to meet them. If you are seeing someone else at present you should consider telling your

Date (if circumstances permit). This would indicate respect for them; you could explain that you would not be with them on a second date if you were not keen, and that of course if the relationship goes further you would cut your other ties.

Family

It is best to say if you have any dependants living with you such as one of your parents or if you have children. You obviously come as a package deal, and it would be misleading to keep silent about them and their influence on your life.

Personal needs

Try to disclose if it is particularly important for you to: live in the country; have a lot of personal space; have lots of company; keep cats; live luxuriously; have children one day; go to discos every other night; have time to pursue your hobbies which may take you away from time to time; run 10 miles before breakfast every day. This will all help you and your Date in future conversations as well as ascertaining your compatibility.

What should you expect sexually?

I feel it is a mistake to expect sex on the second date. If you are to have a lasting relationship, it is generally better to get to know each other for a few dates before bringing sex into the equation. Always have condoms with you in case you do have sex. If you really don't want sex but your Date does, then if he/she is keen enough they will wait. If they can't then this could indicate that maybe their interest in you is purely sexual.

THE SECOND DATE

You have had a successful first date hurdle and now you've arrived at the second. You know enough about the other person to have made you keen to get this far; now you need to learn even more about each other if your friendship is to become a relationship. Think of this date as being divided into four sections.

> ***Four sections of the second date***
>
> - Greeting
> - Relaxing
> - Third degree!
> - Closure and Clinch

Greeting

When you meet this time you can be more familiar than on your first date, and give a continental kiss on both cheeks and a wide open smile. Chat about general topics such as how was the journey, how cold it is today, how lovely they look tonight. You are chatting in a non threatening way to give yourselves time to feel at ease with each other. Remember your body language and try to appear relaxed and attentive, with a happy expression on your face. Once you feel at ease you can move onto the next stage.

Relaxing

In this period you are mentioning all the similarities you like about each other. For example, how good it is that they like going to museums; how pleased you were to hear that are also keen on playing tennis; how excited you are that they like classical music and going to concerts. Hopefully your Date will be as enthusiastic as you are, and you will learn a little more about their feelings for you but remember not to go too over the top. Now you are relaxed, prepare yourself to enter the third degree!

Third degree!

This is the time when you are asking general questions about the other person and their pursuits, which will hopefully open up sufficient intimate details about them to enable you to gauge whether they would like to take the relationship further. From what you are told, you will have a better idea as to whether you wish to proceed as well. You should also try to divulge a little more about yourself and your personal needs to find out if they are acceptable to the other person. All this information is best found out now, rather than taking the risk of getting hurt later.

Closure and Clinch

When it comes to the bill, if you were not the invitee offer to pay your share. If it is refused, and you wish to continue the relationship further, suggest you take them out next time. If you have enjoyed yourself and are still keen on the other person, tell them and ask if they feel the same way. If they don't, then thank them for the enjoyable times you've had together and get back to your drawing board *toute de suite*. However if they are keen - well done! You are hopefully at the start of a promising new relationship.

CHAPTER 7

TAKING THE RELATIONSHIP FURTHER

(HOW FAR CAN YOU GO, AND KEEP IT GOING?)

You have had a few dates and want to take the relationship further, so let's decide what to do next. If you truly find each other attractive and enjoy doing the same things, the limits, as to where you could take your relationship, are boundless. There are no set rules as to how you travel along this road as everyone is unique, but there can be certain guidelines to take into consideration.

PROGRESSING THE RELATIONSHIP

Five factors to bear in mind

- Find common interests

- Go with the flow

- When to take your first trip away

- How to deal with problems

- When to trust

Find common interests

It can be a real burden if every time you want to go out with each other you have to think of new things of interest to do. The ideal is to find a common point of interest to pursue, for example, you may both like giving dinner parties. Consider all of the activities involved with this: deciding on the location (whose home?); preparing the

Taking the Relationship Further

guest list (who to invite?); deciding on the menu (are there any special dietary requirements?); buying the food (where to find the best quality and price?); doing the cooking (who is the better cook?); laying the table, serving the food and drinks and clearing up (not many like these aspects of the party).

You can imagine from all of this what a lot you would have gone through together to arrange a successful dinner party: the in depth discussions (who might get on with who?), compromises (such as choosing a food which your partner and guests like but you don't) and decisions (will we have it this week or next?). Such an exercise would be bound to bring you closer together, enabling you to really get to know each other much better - or it could make you realise your incompatibility!

You can, of course, apply this logic to other activities such as driving in the countryside: whose car will you go in?; who will drive?; which route will you take?; will you stop for food and where?; will you have a picnic? (who prepares this and what will it consist of?); will you stop at a restaurant or pub and should you book?; who will pay for the petrol or food?

It is very important to share responsibilities equally. If one of you always gets landed with making the arrangements, paying, or doing all the hard work, resentments could build up which might stunt your progress. Pursuing activities which only one of you wants to do can get very one sided. It is important to make a fair and equal choice in activities that you are undertaking together. Never take anyone for granted. Gradually you will find that the more things you do together the more relaxed you will become, and you may eventually progress to mentioning activities which you have always wanted to do but never done before – hot air ballooning, clay pigeon shooting, scuba diving, go-karting. If your partner is willing to try these things with you, a whole new world of interests could open up for you both.

Go with the flow

- How often should you see each other

- When to have sex

How often should you see each other

If you are lucky enough to have common interests and you both get caught up in pursuing these, just go with the flow. By this I mean it is not necessary to abide by any specific rules as to how many times you should go out together. If you are both really eager to see each other, I don't personally think that the other person will become keener if you deliberately declined certain dates (because you felt that this was the right game to play); it might in fact have the opposite effect and make them go off the boil.

However, it is probably preferable to avoid overwhelming the other person by trying to fill up every available space in their diary too soon, as you could damage the relationship by appearing to be too keen. This is especially so if they don't appear to be as enthusiastic as you at first; some people prefer a challenge to a pushover so take things steadily until you are sure you both feel the same way. Try not to expect too much too soon from your partner. Just because you may have particular values and habits does not mean that they are the only acceptable ones, and you should not expect others to automatically conform to your standards. We all behave differently, and you need time to get to know each other's individualities.

When to have sex
Again, go with the flow and have sex when you feel relaxed and secure enough in your relationship together. It is important not to expect too much the first time you get together. Both of you will probably be over anxious to perform well and also worried you may disappoint the other. It takes time to get to know and understand each other's sexual needs and this doesn't just happen overnight. Everyone behaves differently, and it is best not to expect your partner to react in any specific way because that is what you are used to. Try not to be difficult or demanding, but just have fun and enjoy the excitement of learning how to achieve a great new sex life together. Let the intimacy of snuggling in bed and telling each other private secrets, be an enjoyable way of progressing your relationship forward both mentally and physically.

When to take your first trip away
Eventually one of you may suggest an activity which involves going away together, such as skiing, sailing or visiting a distant restaurant which would involve an

overnight stay. My advice would always be to have short breaks to start with which only involve one night's stay away. Such short breaks will gradually allow you to get to know each other intimately before embarking on a long stay. You might even consider taking these early breaks with friends, who would act as a foil should any disagreements develop between you.

It is an unfortunate fact of life that many relationships break up after the first holiday away together, probably because they hadn't taken time to learn about each other's differences. It is therefore *vital* 'to go slowly' to get to know each other's annoying habits: leaving wet towels on the floor; squeezing the toothpaste from the top; not hanging clothes up (so you trip over them as you try to find the bed); filling the bathroom shelves with face creams, perfumes and make up; cutting toenails onto the bedroom carpet; snoring – the list is endless.

Another cause of break-ups after the first holiday is often because one person turns out to be a compulsive doer whilst the other doesn't want to do anything at all. It is usually a recipe for disaster when one person's ideal is to wake up early for a swim before a hearty breakfast, then play sports solidly or sight-see until dinner; before dancing the night away in the disco. Whilst the other person just wants to stay in bed late, sunbathe and eat.

To avoid such disasters, it is essential to plan ahead and be open and honest about each other's holiday needs. If you find that one of you prefers to be energetic whilst the other wants to flop out – then compromise. Spend time together brainstorming ideas of what you could both do. For example you could: visit the sights in the morning;

sunbathe and sleep in the afternoon (the energetic one can swim or walk); dine at different restaurants and dance in the disco on alternate nights (making sure that after a late night you have a relaxing snuggle in bed together next morning!)

I must urge you to think carefully about a holiday away if your partner is a heavy drinker and you are not. From personal experience I can tell you that if you do not share the same interest, it can be miserable spending time with someone who only wants to prop up the bar drinking themselves senseless all night and nursing a hangover the next day.

How to deal with problems

The best way to deal with any problem is to tackle it as soon as it arises. If you leave the problem to fester in your mind, even the smallest dilemma will eventually manifest itself as Mount Everest. If someone or something upsets you then say so at once in a non threatening and reasonable manner. Always talk through your problems, and don't stop until explanations have been explored on both sides and both of you are happy with the outcome. Never close the subject with one of you feeling hard done by. If you don't let the other person know you are unhappy about something, a very uncomfortable atmosphere can build up and have a far more destructive effect than any sharp words uttered early on.

A friend of mine once went out with someone who would go silent (sometimes for days) when something she did had upset him. The atmosphere would get worse, and try as she might to get him to say what was the matter, he would say there was nothing wrong. Eventually after three days of such a situation, he arrived home late one night and went straight to bed in silence. She had worked herself up into a nervous frenzy, and picking up the soda siphon (luckily avoiding choosing the carving knife) she stormed into the bedroom and squirted it at her sleeping boyfriend. He and the bed were soaked, and during the ensuing argument she learnt what she had done *wrong* three days before! What a lot of nervous tension, time and energy could have been saved if he had spoken out at the beginning.

Six problems that could arise

- Friends
- Jealousy
- Children
- Body clocks
- Personal habits
- Pets

Friends

You can choose your own friends but unfortunately you can't choose your partner's. It is important not to try to influence their friendships because this could lead to resentment towards you and a closer bonding with their friend. Tolerance is the key word here. If you really don't like any of your partner's friends, spend enough time with them so as not to appear to be rude and then occupy yourself elsewhere. Try not to complain about them to your partner, but if pressed for an explanation as to why you avoid spending time with their friend be honest about how you feel – but also emphasise that it is not a criticism of them. Explain that you are happy for them to spend time with their friend but you would rather be elsewhere.

If your relationship means more than their friendship, your partner will appreciate your feelings and accept the situation. If they insist that you spend most of your free time with people that you do not get on with, then you must think long and hard as to whether this relationship is the right one for you, and whether you both have enough similar interests in life.

Jealousy

Jealousy is an insecurity in yourself, making you feel that others are more important you are, and that you are worth a lesser amount of love than them. Try to recognise that jealousy is a put down of yourself and that you don't need the love and approval of others to give you a sense of value. Being jealous is allowing someone else's behaviour to cause you emotional discomfort. It is a wasted emotion which prevents you from enjoying the present moment.

If you really loved yourself, you would not allow yourself to get upset if your partner chooses to look at or spend time with someone else. It is their choice and absolutely no reflection on you or your worth. Jealousy cannot alter a situation to your advantage, but may well have the reverse affect of driving your partner away. Jealousy is a lack of trust in the other person, and without trust no relationship can survive.

It is important to remember that you are human beings. That means you will both find some people you meet attractive, even though you may be deeply in love with each other. So long as you *look but don't touch* no harm is done. However, you would be foolish to deliberately try to make your partner feel that something is going on – in order to make them feel insecure – as you could damage your relationship and destroy their trust in you.

You have a responsibility towards your partner to minimise the possibility of making them feel insecure; even the most easy going partner, if pushed to the extreme, can get jealous. If you find that your partner's behaviour is causing you to feel unnecessarily insecure however hard you try to control your emotions, then you must discuss the problem together, calmly and rationally, without throwing out any accusations.

If the problem cannot be resolved through discussion, consider seeking professional help to see if the problem is fundamental within you, or reconsider whether you are in the right relationship. If you both care enough for each other, there is no way that either of you would want to inflict emotional distress on the other. If either of you unwittingly did so, you would take great pains to reassure the other and also try to make sure that such a situation never occurred again. A good relationship is priceless and worth nurturing, and it would be foolish to put it at risk by playing silly games.

Sometimes a relationship begins with one person still carrying excess baggage in the form of predatory ex- boyfriends/girlfriends. However flattering it may be to have the attention of such people, or reassuring to have the security of keeping them on the sidelines should the relationship go wrong, excess baggage will always disrupt and may finally destroy even the most understanding of relationships. On the other hand, if you feel bothered by your partner's ex and your partner reassures you that there is nothing more than friendship between them, always including you when they meet up, then try to accept what they say. If you can't, then maybe you don't trust your partner and should consider whether to continue with the relationship.

Children

If your partner has children from a previous relationship you have to accept them as a package deal, and make an effort (as the adult intruding into their home and lifestyle) to make friends with them. This will necessitate a lot of understanding and tolerance of their possible resentment towards you, on your behalf and should be something you discuss at an early stage with your partner. It is in both your interests that you fit comfortably into their family life and you need to tackle each problem as it arises together.

Children are very protective of their parents, especially if they have seen them hurt in the past and they will need some winning over. Never make the mistake of trying to become a surrogate mother/father; they already have a real mother and father and would resent your intrusion. Also avoid being a people pleaser, by giving in to whatever they want just to win their affection; this is unlikely to work in the end. Instead try to become a friend and confidant, someone they can talk to when it is difficult for them to discuss their problems with their parents. In short, someone who is not a pushover and with whom they can have fun.

If having tried your best to be friends with the children and they are still hostile towards you, discuss the problem with your partner to try to find a solution. It may take time but, provided the parents exert enough discipline and control over their offspring and give them lots of love and attention, if you really want the relationship to work, you will win through in the end.

Body clocks

Some of us are better in the morning and some of us late at night. If this causes a problem between you, it is something that should have been taken into consideration before you even thought of going out with each other. If the problem only comes to light once you really spend a lot of time with each other, you must discuss the problem together and compromise. Maybe you can agree to have late nights at the weekends when you can have a lie in the next day, and get to bed early during the week. Although it is difficult to do, if your relationship means enough to you, you can adjust your body clock to different timings. You can change any aspect of yourself if you have the will to do so and you feel the relationship is worth it.

Personal habits

Everyone has habits that others may not like and you have to be able to compromise if you want a pleasant existence together. Discuss what habits annoy you both, and maybe trade them off by giving up some of yours in exchange for your partner giving up some of theirs.

Sometimes shock tactics work. If your partner never clears up after themselves, leaves dirty cups and plates around and throws their belongings on the floor for you to tidy up – stop doing it and see what happens. Hopefully, they will be bewildered at first and wonder what is happening. Eventually they may get fed up with their own mess and begin tidying up after themselves. On no account fall back into the old habit of clearing up after them. Of course you do take a risk if you follow this advice of being dropped in favour of another slave to clean up after them. If this happens, I think you would be well rid of them.

Sometimes when your partner's irritating habits really get on your nerves, it is worth taking time to reflect on their good points. If some of the good and loving acts they do for you, often uninvited, outweigh the bad, maybe you can learn to be more tolerant After all none of us is perfect.

Pets

So long as you don't have an allergy to a particular animal such as cats, and they are not allowed to intrude into your general well being, try your best to tolerate your partner's pet. Before you came on the scene this animal was probably their best friend and companion, and it would be unfair to expect them to throw their nearest and dearest out because you don't like it.

However, if the animal is allowed to intrude into your life by constantly messing up your home with its dirty paws, or if you are not able to go anywhere without taking it with you, or you have to sleep in bed with it and constantly listen to your partner chat to their pet, then you will be justified in feeling irritated. Again, please discuss the problem together and compromise. Maybe there should be certain areas of the house such as the bedroom where the animal is not allowed. Maybe the animal can be paid for to be looked after by someone else at various times when you don't want it with you. Maybe your partner can have discussions with their pet when you are out of earshot.

When to trust

You must give your partner the benefit of your trust from the very beginning of your relationship. They are less likely to betray your trust if you are not fearful of them doing so.

Sometimes when we are deeply in love and really happy with someone, we get so fearful of losing them that we unwittingly sabotage our own relationship in varying ways. We may always look for negative signs that things are going wrong with the relationship rather than dwelling on all the positive aspects, this may well depress the most easy going of partners until they *just* see the negative and the relationship falls apart. When the relationship eventually goes wrong we will have been proved right, because we knew deep down it was too good to last. The stupid thing is that if we had not been fearful and panicked, the outcome would probably have been the opposite. Fear will always attract the negative towards you. Trusting and imagining a happy ending will attract a positive outcome.

At some point in your relationship, if things are still going really well for you both, you will probably consider whether you should commit yourself; by this I mean whether you should live together or get married. It is one thing to share your partner's home with them whilst keeping on your own as a bolt hole should things go wrong between you, quite another to sell up and share a mortgage together. You have to be really sure in your own mind that this relationship is right for you, before you involve your finances. Financial bickering and problems can destroy the strongest of relationships.

Living together
Living together is sometimes less threatening and claustrophobic to those who are fearful of losing their freedom. Not feeling tied down, and feeling able to walk out at any time should things go wrong (without legal complications), is a comforting way to live for some. If you both feel the same way, then this is the ideal situation for you. However, it can be far too easy to just walk out when problems arise, rather than working them through; there always seems to be a get-out clause.

Of course, some people may live together as a trial period before committing to marriage or having children. This could turn out to be a recipe for disaster. If one partner wants the commitment of marriage whilst the other doesn't see the point of upsetting the apple cart once they have been living together for a while. The partner who wishes to marry may gradually feel insecure and lose confidence in the relationship, which could create strife and unhappiness for both of them.

Getting married

Many people believe that getting married is the ultimate commitment you can make to a relationship, and is a public declaration of your love and dedication to your partner. However, you must be sure that this is the right step for you, and that you will not feel trapped and claustrophobic once you have signed on the dotted line. It is very easy to get married, but traumatic and costly to get divorced should things go wrong. Also, do not get married just because of a pregnancy. An unhappy home would be far worse for the child than being born out of wedlock. You and the new baby are the most important people to consider. However, having weighed up all the pros and cons, if you are prepared to make the effort to discuss and work out any difficulties between you, and to devote yourself to your partner's happiness for better or for worse, this could be the best and most rewarding decision of your life.

MAINTAINING THE RELATIONSHIP

Five aspects to consider in keeping the relationship going

- Romance
- Communication
- Staying friends
- Boredom
- Attraction to others

Romance

If love makes the world go round, then it could be said that romance lubricates the bearings, and in my opinion you can never have too much of it! Romance can be any little act that surprises, delights, titillates and makes the other person feel good. A romantic act does not have to be an extravagant gesture such as whisking your loved one away for an unexpected Valentines night dinner in Paris. It can be a simple gesture such as: a gift of a single rose; a phone call to say 'I love you'; a candlelit dinner at home; cuddling up in front of a log fire on a winter's night; 'holding hands at midnight under a starry sky' to make your loved one feel special.

It is important to make regular payments into your emotional bank account. By this I mean instead of once a year maybe giving a red rose, going out for a romantic dinner for two, or saying 'I love you', you should frequently do romantic deeds which will always keep the emotional bank account topped up and in credit.

Communication

It is vital to constantly communicate with each other, talking through the good times, the problems and the worries. To do this you need to make an effort to spend time together. Nowadays there is so much to occupy our time such as: working to make ends meet; looking after a family or pursuing a hobby, that we sometimes lose track of our priorities and neglect our partner. It is essential to make time for each other to avoid drifting apart.

Communication by touch is also an essential element of any relationship. Sometimes a reassuring arm around the shoulder or a kiss can speak more than a thousand words.

Remember that your relationship should never stand still or be taken for granted. Strive to improve it at all times through the learning process of communication, negotiation and compromise. Maybe every few months sit down together and discuss how to re-evaluate your relationship. Set new guide lines because not only is life around us constantly changing, we are too.

Staying friends

It is difficult to have a loving and fulfilling relationship with your partner unless there is a deep, underlying friendship between you.

Good friends like and trust each other, treat one another in a courteous way and respect the other's feelings. They respect each other's individuality, do not take liberties with them and allow them to be their own person whether or not their views coincide with their own. Being friends with someone is being able to say sorry when you are in the wrong, being able to wait for your friend to say sorry to you and accepting that apology with good grace. Genuine friends will listen to each other's aims and aspirations, praise, support, encourage them, and pick them up if things go wrong. Friends like making each other happy, and having fun and laughs together. They will try to think of ways to please their friend and try to avoid undermining the other's confidence with unhealthy criticisms. Finally, friends are a united team who will stand by each other whatever circumstances may try to dictate.

Boredom

Boredom is debilitating and unhealthy and it is important to keep any relationship exciting and interesting, trying not to fall into boring routine habits. Anything can become boring if it becomes a routine habit, even buying your partner a bunch of flowers each week can lose its novelty value. Try to think of new things to do and please – variety is the spice of life. Someone once told me that boring people get bored. People who are not boring would never allow themselves the self-indulgence of getting bored. They will always find something to do to amuse themselves or others.

Be original in your thinking and don't expect your partner to provide all the inspiration. If you hear your partner mention that there is a particular film or show they would like to see, present them with surprise tickets one evening. Arrange a weekend away to somewhere they have always wanted to visit, suggest learning a new sport or dance together, suggest some home improvements which you could tackle together such as decorating. Try to keep interesting projects on the go, keep abreast of the news, maintain individual interests such as your work or a hobby as well as sharing activities together and you will always have lots to talk about. Try to avoid being like many couples who sit together in silence in a restaurant, seemingly having nothing left to say to each other except pleasantries such as, 'What would you like for your main course?'

Keep your sense of humour and try to see the ridiculous and absurd in almost any situation and have a laugh together. Keeping your partner amused will make them feel good and hopefully keep depressing boredom at bay.

Keep your sex life stimulating and exciting and don't fall into boring routines. Surprise your lover with ingenuity such as making love in unusual places, anywhere so long as it's not too uncomfortable, will do! Make love in the shower, in the bath, on the stairs, under the stars, by candlelight, in front of a log fire on a winter's night. Read a few books on the subject or watch films that you find erotic and sexy if you run out of ideas. Try to keep your passion as spontaneous and alive as when you first lusted after each other.

Attraction to others
Be satisfied with what you have and never jeopardise it for the sake of a fleeting fling. A good relationship is priceless and worthy of a lot of effort to keep it in good shape. The grass doesn't usually turn out to be any greener if you stray, and you run the risk of losing something very precious. Try not to put yourself in the way of temptation by going on holiday or to a party on your own. There will always be predatory, unattached people around who would delight in stealing you away from your happy relationship. Look at others when you are with your partner and thank your lucky stars you have each other.

CHAPTER 8

DATING FROM SCRATCH IN LATER LIFE

(IT NEEDN'T BE AN ITCHY PROBLEM!)

You're older, wiser, possibly wealthier, so theoretically life should be a lot easier but, once again you're back on that shelf. Well don't fret and imagine you are too rusty to start the cogs spinning smoothly around again: all you need is a quick refresher course and a bit of a dust down, and you'll be snatched off your perch back into circulation in no time at all. You'll hardly realise that your feet have touched the ground once your 'second time around' dating plan has been put into action.

> *The Second Time Around Dating Plan*
>
> - Mentally shake yourself up
>
> - Get yourself back into shape
>
> - Plan your "come back" and throw yourself into life ASAP

Mentally Shake yourself up

Sorting your mind out in preparation for dating in later life is no different to that described in the first chapter of this book. However there are a certain areas which I believe deserve a closer look at.

> *Three topics to be carefully considered*
>
> - Confidence building
>
> - Getting to know yourself
>
> - Changing your attitudes

Confidence building

Starting from scratch again, especially in later life is a shock to anyone's system. The fact that you may be experiencing a total lack of confidence in yourself, feeling insecure and generally off balance for maybe the first time in your life, is not surprising. A relationship break up is very similar to a bereavement and you must be kind and understanding to yourself, and realise that you need and must undergo a grieving period in order to achieve balance in your life again. Allow yourself a period of time to lick your wounds and discuss your feelings with friends or a professional counsellor and remember that time is a great healer. However, there has to be a mental deadline when you say to yourself 'Enough of all this, I am now going to get on with the rest of my life.' No regrets, no recriminations, just a positive attitude that you are about to make your life change for the better.

First of all you must understand that although you may be recovering from a broken relationship, this does not mean that you are a failure. I firmly believe that most things happen for a purpose, therefore, because things did not work out at a particular time with a particular person probably means you were destined to meet someone else with whom you will be far happier. If you can learn to treat every set back as a useful learning process, this will enrich you as a person and increase your chances of success with whomsoever life has destined for you.

You have to kiss a lot of frogs before you meet your prince/princess!

It sometimes takes a while to feel comfortable being single again if you have been in a relationship for a long time. A friend of mine used to feel dizzy whenever she left her wedding ring off after her marriage broke up. It was a prop for her, and she somehow felt less of a person in public without it. She used to practice walking round her house for a few hours each day without wearing the ring, until one day she eventually realised that her feelings of inadequacy were just in her mind. Other people didn't think any less of her because she was single, in fact most were more interested because she was once more a free agent. Be proud of being single again and being able to choose for yourself with whom and what you would like to be doing. You will be surprised how many people in relationships which are less than perfect, envy your position.

Never think you are over the hill or past it. You only have to look at statistics to know that there are countless others of a similar age in the same predicament, probably with the same feelings as yourself. A person's appeal to another comes from within. An optimistic, youthful and enquiring mind, and a happy and carefree disposition in later years will be strong competition for just youthful looks. You are just as attractive and desirable as you have always been, only you have to accept this yourself. Always remember that you are unique and therefore a very special person. You deserve to be loved and treated well because you are you and should always settle for nothing less. Never be desperate for just any new relationship in order to justify your worth to others. Recognise how worthy you are and bide your time until you meet someone who is worthy of you.

Recognise your achievements and plus points by writing them all down. If you give yourself enough time to think of everything, you will be surprised how impressive that list will look. Give yourself some mental praise and vow never to sell yourself short again. Always try to think and say positive things about yourself, and always talk positively about others. Never be tempted to say negative things about your ex. You will gain more admiration by keeping your dignity and only saying good things.

We all have insecurities but some of us are more adept at hiding them than others. Put on a brave face, look happy and act out a confident role. You will find in no time at all that your act soon becomes a reality.

Getting to know yourself

Chances are that you have been so wrapped up in thinking about another person's needs and pleasures and also your children's (if you have any), that you have forgotten your own. You probably don't know yourself or your own personal needs any more and have forgotten what gives you enjoyment. Sometimes if two people are together for a long time they cease to behave as individuals and become mirror images of each other. Consequently should their relationship break up they feel more disorientated than most because they have 'lost' part of their personality. Learn to be your own person again - a unique individual with special needs and qualities of your own. This is an exciting time for you - a voyage of re-discovery!

Get some paper and a pen and list everything you can remember that you have ever enjoyed. Delve back in your mind (to your childhood if necessary), and list games, hobbies, work, activities, people and places. Having made this list, make another about what you have always wanted to do and where you have always wanted to visit. Armed with these two lists you should have a better self portrait of yourself than before. Now is the time for you; there's not a moment to waste. Every moment is precious so you might as well start enjoying each one. Look at your list of achievements and attributes and appreciate what you have to offer the world.

Changing your attitudes

You can't change others but you can change yourself and your attitudes. If your life so far has not gone the way you would have wished, then now is an ideal time for change. Don't be world weary and think *I can't go through all this again.* Of course you can! Life is an adventure which should be embraced, set backs and all, until the end of your days.

Learn to be happy with yourself and accept who you are. Remember that nothing in this life is perfect, including yourself, and try to be less critical of yourself and others. Have the courage to do or say whatever you like, providing you don't upset anyone in the process, and don't be afraid of what others may think of you. Decide what you want to be not the way others want you to be. Love and respect yourself and you will find that others will mirror your opinion.

Make time for yourself and down shift if necessary to give yourself the maximum opportunity to enjoy every moment of your life. Always imagine a successful outcome to anything you do and block out negative thoughts. Let your vocabulary be filled with the words *I can* and *I shall*. Change your negative patterns so that you avoid: being stressed; always in a mess, always late or always feeling tired and unwell. If you have the will to do so, you will always find the way.

Take responsibility for everything that happens in your life. You can't change the way others behave towards you – but you can walk away if they make you feel unhappy. If anything is causing you distress it is within your power to change, avoid or eliminate that stress from your life.

Think about the sort of person you would ideally like to meet but be sure your ideas are not too fixed or rigid. Throw away those mental check lists and be more flexible and learn from past mistakes. If you have always gone for the same type, maybe that type isn't right for you.

Don't put the responsibility of your own personal happiness on to someone else....

Get yourself back into shape

The most important thing to achieve is a healthy active body which you feel comfortable with. Don't think you have to pump iron in the gym at every available moment to re-capture the figure of your youth. Ideally, start a healthy regime of exercising three times a week either in the gym, swimming pool or playing a sport such as tennis or golf. But remember, once is better than not at all.

Also train yourself to eat a more healthy diet of fresh foods, cut down on the alcohol intake, stop smoking and get enough sleep. In this way you will increase your muscle tone and improve your complexion and any ageing lines considerably. If you have the time and finances to do so, pamper yourself with a stay at a health farm to give you a good head start.

Consider changing your image to perk your spirits up. A new hairstyle or new wardrobe will often do wonders for your self image and confidence. However, do not try to disguise your age by dressing up as 'medallion man' or 'mutton dressed as lamb.' This will not do you any favours in your search for a new Date. Be yourself.

Finally, have regular medical and dental check ups so that you know you are in fighting form when you re-launch yourself back into the social whirl.

Plan your 'come back' and throw yourself into life ASAP

Your objective is to create as many opportunities as you can to meet other unattached people, form new friendships and meet a special Date.

Three areas to consider

- Leisure pursuits
- Work
- Agencies/Adverts

Leisure pursuits

It is a sad fact of life that when a relationship breaks up, 'friends' disappear at the same time. Many people find it difficult to cope with split loyalties and decide to side with one partner or abandon ship altogether. If you find yourself deserted by so-called friends, then take heart that you are not alone in your situation. You now have a golden opportunity to enrich your life with new friends and possibly join a completely new social circle. Now is the time to decide about the type of person you most enjoy being with and seriously think about where they might frequent. Most people will participate in some leisure activity whether it is physical or mental, and unattached people have more time than most to do this so you are bound to meet them somewhere.

Consult your lists of what you would like to do and start putting some of your ideas in motion. Whether you are learning a new sport, studying a language at night school or joining a dance class, you will be meeting new people who share the same interest. You will immediately broaden your horizons and add a new spark of interest to your daily routine. Consider the many holidays, weekend breaks and outings which are on offer for single people. Health farms are also good environments for meeting other single people, providing social and sports activities as well as licking you into shape.

Work

Maybe you have worked at home so far as a housewife and mother. Many women feel intense feelings of guilt towards their children when the marriage breaks up, and think they should spend even more time with them than before to soften the blow. Very often this makes the situation at home more stressful if the children play on her guilt feelings and become more demanding and she is given no respite. In these circumstances it is far more beneficial to the family as a whole for the mother to go out to work and have a change of scene and meet other adults. If you are in this position, so long as you can arrange for adequate child care whilst you are away from home, the break from household routines will provide a better quality of life both mentally and financially for all of you. You will make friends at work who in turn may introduce you to a world of new activities and interests.

If you are already employed and truly wish to change your circumstances then why not consider asking for a transfer to another region or change jobs. Changing yourself, your lifestyle and your place of work can only open up new hitherto unsuspected opportunities to widen your social scene.

Agencies/Adverts

Finding a Date in later years can be difficult if the only people you associate with have partners, with no single friends to introduce you to. You probably don't relish frequenting clubs, pubs and wine bars on your own to pick up or be picked up, so what do you do? If you're not sporty, interested in joining evening classes or societies you might like to consider enlisting the help of Dating Agencies or Dining and Social Events Clubs. Both will introduce you to other unattached people of a similar age and hopefully similar interests, and are a convenient way to help you re-organise your social life. With a Dating Agency you will date a stranger on a one to one basis which might be daunting to some, and with a Dining and Social Events Club you will meet a group of strangers at once whilst enjoying a dinner party or event at the same time. Both have their merits, it is up to you to decide your preference.

Whatever you decide, do be careful that you choose a reputable company and do not part with large sums of money in the desperate hope that this will enhance your chances of meeting a rich partner. Finding your ideal Date is nothing but a numbers game; the more people you meet, the more chance you have of meeting Mr or Ms Right. No-one can guarantee to introduce you to them because there is always that hidden 'X' factor which no-one can account for.

If you decide to place an advert or reply to one in the personal columns, do be careful. However old or experienced we are, we can all be taken in by someone if we feel at a low ebb. Your Date has not been vetted by a middle contact so always meet in a public place and listen to your inner instincts. On the plus side you will get lots of dates and this could build up your confidence as you learn to meet many people on an individual basis again.

Advantages of Dating in Later Life

However downhearted you may feel at the prospect of starting the dating game all over again at a period in your life when ideally you would like to be comfortably settled with the partner of your choice, let's look at the plus side of this situation.

Three positive aspects of dating in later years

- Release from an unhappy situation

- Better chance for real happiness

- More experience and less hang ups

Release from an unhappy situation

Like many others, you may have been locked into an unhappy situation for a long time with no prospect of a happy solution, feeling too afraid of the unknown to make a break. Hopefully, now you realise that fear of the unknown is far worse than the reality. You are now a free agent able to exercise your imagination to make a wish list and with enough determination to make those wishes come true.

Better chance for real happiness

You now have the potential to make yourself happier than you have ever been in your life before. Having learned from past mistakes you should have a much better idea of what you want and the type of person you feel most comfortable with, than you would have had when you were younger. Armed with this knowledge you have the chance to meet someone of a similar age and experience, with interests and aspirations which coincide with your own. If you throw yourself into it with enthusiasm, you will be surprised how this new adventure in life will make you feel more youthful and energetic, and that in turn will do wonders for your appearance. Without the tie of responsibility towards an unhappy partnership, you now have the freedom to make any dream come true. Let your imagination run wild. Even if you only achieve half of your wishes that will be 100% better than what you had before. You were born into this world to live, so you might as well live life to the full. Enjoy every moment, recapture your sense of humour and spoil yourself - you deserve it.

More experience and less hang ups

You will have experienced many of life's ups and downs and will hopefully be more tolerant and understanding of other's failings, and recognise the value of compromise and negotiation. You will have the confidence of finally knowing what makes you happy and therefore not waste your valuable time on unsuitable liaisons. Having gained more experience you will be better able to communicate to a potential partner your needs and aspirations. If you have gained knowledge from your former mistakes you will have less hang ups and be able to cope better with any baggage you might have picked up along the way. You will have learned the true value of friendship and trust as opposed to lust and playing games, which will lead to a deeper more meaningful partnership next time.

With both feet set firmly on the ground, you will find love is far lovelier the second time around!

Conclusion

People and relationships are so complex that there can never be a magic set of rules to ensure that you meet and then attract your ideal partner. Although the guidelines I have suggested in this book will help you to find the right pathway, you must always use your own intuition as to whether or not you are on route.

Use this book as your Guide but remember that above all you must always be yourself. Be proud of yourself and never take offence if your affections are unrequited. Always treat rejection as a useful stepping stone and learning stage on your journey to find the right choice for you. Be relaxed and happy with your life, enjoy every moment and never fall into the desperate trap of trying to meet the 'perfect person'. If you follow this advice and the guidelines in this book everything else will fall into place.

About the Author

Through her Agony Aunt pages on the Internet, her own monthly column in *Home & Life* magazine, and her many articles, Hillie answers hundreds of problems every month in her own inimitable, sensible and sympathetic style covering a diverse range of subjects from health to happiness.

Left with two small children after 18 years of marriage, she divorced her husband in 1989 and started Dinner Dates; a leading dining and social events company with over 7,000 members.

In the early days of her Dinner Dates company Hillie hosted every event personally, and her natural warmth and charm led many members to bring her a wide range of personal problems and she became the listening ear to thousands.

Hillie originally trained as a radiographer but left to pursue her interest in music and theatre. She started as an opera singer and later starred in musical comedy, pantomine and plays.

In 1980 she formed her production company Edwardians Unlimited, producing Old Time Music Hall and Variety shows starring such celebrities as Roy Hudd, Barbara Windsor, Nicholas Parsons, Leslie Crowther, Clive Dunn and Barry Cryer. Whenever Hillie can find the time, she still appears in them herself!

Hillie will be familiar to many through her TV appearances on programmes such as the *Esther Rantzen* and *Kilroy* shows, where she contributes her considerable experience on personal, practical and emotional problems.

Other books by Hillie Marshall

Hillie Marshall's Guide to Successful Relationships
Foreword by Nicholas Parsons

The world's first Global Agony Aunt on the Internet, this book will guide people of all ages and both sexes through the complexities of human relationships.

ISBN 1 873475 33 0
USA $9.99   Can $11.99   UK £6.99

Agonise With Hillie
Foreword by Peter Stringfellow

Agonise With Hillie is a riveting anthology of problems from kids, teenagers and adults. From dating through to later life, Hillie has the answers to every aspect of social life.

ISBN 1 873475 80 2
USA $9.99   Can $11.99   UK £6.99

Recommended Further Reading

Men Are From Mars, Women Are From Venus
John Gray Ph.D. (Thorsons)

Your Erroneous Zones
Dr. Wayne W. Dyer (Warner)

Being Happy
Andrew Matthews (Media Masters)